The Deserted Medieval Village of Broadfield, Herts.

Eric C. Klingelhöfer

British Archaeological Reports 2
1974

BRITISH ARCHAEOLOGICAL REPORTS

122, Banbury Road, Oxford OX2 7BP, England

General Editors:

A.R.Hands, B.Sc., M.A., D.Phil.

Mrs Y.M.Hands

D.R.Walker, B.A.

Advisory Editors:

C.B.Burgess, M.A.

Neil Cossons, M.A., F.S.A., F.M.A.

Professor B.W.Cunliffe, M.A., Ph.D., F.S.A.

Sonia Chadwick Hawkes, B.A., M.A., F.S.A.

Professor G.D.B.Jones, M.A., D.Phil., F.S.A.

Frances Lynch, M.A., F.S.A.

P.A.Mellars, M.A., Ph.D.

P.A.Rahtz, M.A., F.S.A.

<u>B.A.R.</u> 2, 1974: "Broadfield"   © Eric C. Klingelhöfer, 1974

ISBN 9780904531015 paperback
ISBN 9781407319346 e-book
DOI https://doi.org/10.30861/9780904531015
A catalogue record for this book is available from the British Library
This book is available at www.barpublishing.com

BROADFIELD

CONTENTS

Page

LIST OF ILLUSTRATIONS

I.   SUMMARY   1

II.   INTRODUCTION   1

III.   DOCUMENTARY EVIDENCE   3

IV.   TOPOGRAPHY OF THE VILLAGE   6

V.   THE EXCAVATIONS   8

VI.   INTERPRETATION   24

VII.   COMMENTARY   34

VIII.   DESCRIPTION OF FINDS   39

ABBREVIATIONS FOR APPENDICES   63

APPENDIX A: CHRONOLOGICAL REFERENCES TO
             BROADFIELD ESTATES   64

APPENDIX B: CHRONOLOGICAL REFERENCES TO
             BROADFIELD AND RUSHDEN CHURCHES   67

APPENDIX C: ILLUSTRATED POTTERY TABLE   69

APPENDIX D: A NOTE ON THROCKING CHURCH   71

BIBLIOGRAPHY   72

LIST OF ILLUSTRATIONS

FIGURES   Page

1. Topography of Broadfield Parish   2
2. Broadfield D. M. V.   7
3. Site Plan. 1965   9
4. Plan of East Platform   11
5. Plan of West Platform   15
6. Section of Churchyard Ditch, Trench J   15
7. Sections of Church Site   facing   16
8. Plan of Pre - Church Features   19
9. Plan of Church Features   21
10. Interpretation of West Platform   25
11. Interpretation of Church Site   29
12. Site Interpretation, Period I   31
13. Site Interpretation, Period II   33
14. Hertfordshire Deserted Medieval Villages   38
15. Worked Stone, Roof Tiles, Other Fired Clay, and Bronze   41
16. Illustrated Pottery No. 1   45
17. Illustrated Pottery No. 2   47
18. Illustrated Pottery No. 3   49
19. Illustrated Pottery No. 4   51
20. Illustrated Pottery No. 5   53
21. Illustrated Pottery No. 6   55
22. Stained Glass and Iron   57

PLATES   facing 22

Ia. Broadfield Church from the east, excavated to buried soil, layer 15.
Ib. Sanctuary step and grave, F. 9, from the west.

Please note that additional material is available to download from
www.barpublishing.com/additional-downloads.html.

The original foldouts have been reduced in size to match the A4 format of this
book, the images are therefore not as clear as the original foldouts. Please refer
to the original foldouts via the download for the original content.

THE DESERTED MEDIEVAL VILLAGE OF BROADFIELD, HERTS

I. SUMMARY

The deserted medieval village of Broadfield, Herts., was investigated by a rescue excavation in 1965. Trenching revealed multi-period house platforms and hollow ways. Excavation of the parish church revealed a rectangular building 39' by 14', later expanded to 45' by 14', with a period of use from c.1220 to c.1450. Three phases were distinguished: the first with wall benches and graves along the north wall; the second with additions to the wall benches and with graves marked by memorial slabs throughout the nave; and the third with an expansion eastward of the building, a raised sanctuary, and a tile floor in the nave. Its cemetery was well organized, and may have had family enclosures.

The church was built upon earlier peasant crofts, and from the different alignments of the buildings and ditches, a pattern of change in the village plan has been constructed. While the construction of the church destroyed individual houses and crofts, the layout of its enclosure shows that it generally conformed to the original street plan. However, later structures were aligned directly to the church enclosures and a new street plan evolved, aligned to the axis of the church itself.

II. INTRODUCTION

Broadfield Hall (Nat. Grid TL/325312) is located in the northeastern part of Hertfordshire, by the headwaters of the Beane (Fig. 1). Three villages lie close by: Rushden, a mile to the northwest; Cottered, a mile to the southwest; and Throcking, a mile to the southeast. It is on high, open ground, predominantly boulder clay and chalk. The site, lying within and alongside an orchard, consisted of a church enclosure and two adjacent

1

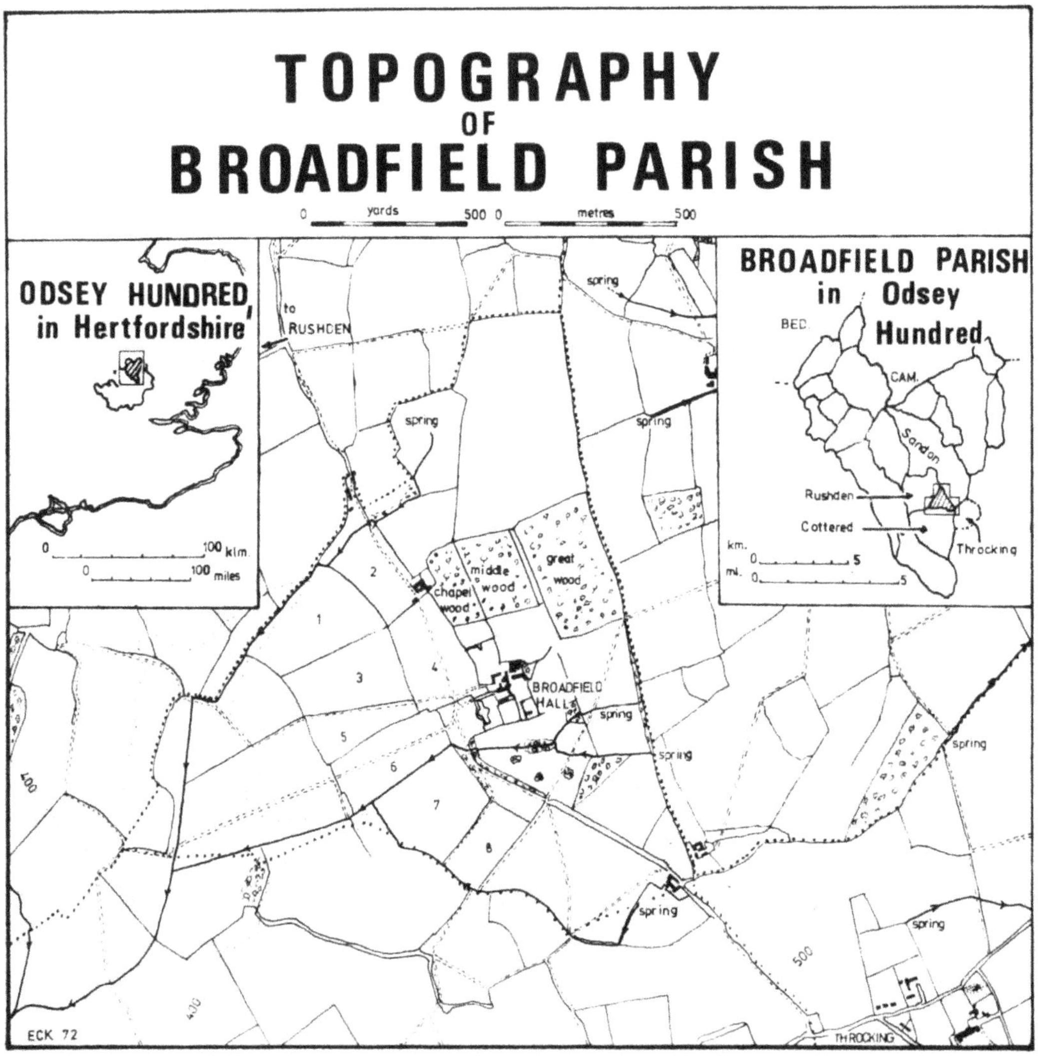
TOPOGRAPHY
OF
BROADFIELD PARISH
0 yards 500 0 metres 500
ODSEY HUNDRED, in Hertfordshire
0 100 klm.
0 100 miles
BROADFIELD PARISH in Odsey Hundred
BED.
CAM.
Sandon
Rushden
Cottered
Throcking
km. 0 5
mi. 0 5
to RUSHDEN
spring
middle wood
chapel wood
great wood
BROADFIELD HALL
THROCKING
ECK 72

Fig. 1

platforms. It was excavated in 1965 by Mr. P. A. Rahtz of the University of Birmingham with students and labourers for the Ministry of Public Buildings and Works (now Department of the Environment). It was a rescue excavation, in advance of agricultural development. Excavation took place for three weeks in April-May and for four weeks in September. After the excavation, the site was deeply ploughed, and today nothing remains to be seen. The finds and records are deposited at the Verulamium Museum, St. Albans, Herts.[1]

III. DOCUMENTARY EVIDENCE

In the documentary evidence there is little or no mention of a Broad-field village per se, but there is reference to the manor and church. One should note a decrease in the size of the manor from its 430 acres at Domesday [Hine 1951, 2] to its present 375 acres. This loss is documented in the several tracts of land separated from Broadfield and given to ecclesiastical foundations.

THE MANOR: The Domesday Book contains the first mention of Broad-field (Bradefella). In 1066 the land was held by two overlords, Queen Edith with 1/2 hide and Stigund, Archbishop of Canterbury, with 2 1/2 hides. Goda was tenant of the queen and Laedmar, Ansgot, and two brothers were men of the archbishop. By 1086 the land had changed hands: Earl Roger of Montgomery had acquired the queen's half hide, while Stigund's lands were divided by three other Norman lords. The land held by Laedmar, one hide and 3/4 virgate, was owned by Sigar de Cioches who held several other estates in Hertfordshire. Ansgot's one hide and 1/4 virgate were owned by Hardwin de Scales, another large landowner. The small estate held by the two brothers passed into the hands of Robert, Bishop of Chester.

[1] I should like to thank Mr. Rahtz for making records and finds available to me; the report was written as an M. A. dissertation at the University of Birmingham. Mr. Rahtz would like to thank Margaret Gray, Howard Clarke, Chris Dyer and Peter Wade-Martins, who supervised the excavations. I should also like to thank all those who have contributed to this report: J.G. Hurst, C.R. Oyler, P.A. Newton, and I. H. Goodall.

It was the holding of Ansgot that became the manor of Broadfield; de Scales' tenant was Theobald, who held several other estates from him in Hertfordshire. Theobald's family (later known as FitzRalph) held Broadfield until 1428, sometimes subleasing it, and the descent of the manor is fairly well documented (see Appendix A). This stable condition ended, however, in the fifteenth century, when after a brief ownership by the Clerk family, the land was an object of frequent transferral and sale. There were eighteen recorded owners or part owners in the next hundred and fifty years, until Edward Pulter reunited the estate in 1592.

The other portions of Broadfield Manor can also be traced. Earl Roger's half hide was apparently inherited by his daughter, Sybil de Raynes, who in 1140 gave land in Rushden to the Knights Hospitallers' preceptory in Shingay, Cambridgeshire. This land was known as Shingay Manor, and survived the Dissolution as the name of a local wood (see Appendix A).

The Bishop of Chester's single virgate was presumably inherited by his relatives, the de Somery earls of Gloucestershire. Their manor of Bygrave, Herts., had attached to it in Edward I's time a park at Broadfield. This single virgate may well have been that which in the fourteenth century was known as Maunseys (sic.), Bradfield, and Cumberlow. This land was, in fact, briefly reunited with Broadfield by the Clerks in 1428, but soon thereafter was divided and by 1602 was part of the manor of Rushden (see Appendix A).

The land owned by Sigar de Cioches is less easy to trace. It is probable that it was attached to the neighbouring manor of Rushden of which he was lord, though there is no documentary evidence to that effect.

Lastly, the lords of Broadfield detached some of their own land. In 1159 thirty acres were granted to the Abbey of Warden, as well as a ten year lease on the manor itself. The grant of thirty acres was later confirmed, and the holding was added to by other local landlords in the thirteenth century. It became Broadfield Grange or Friars' Grange, the latter name at present attached to a farm and wood north of Broadfield (see Appendix A).

THE CHURCH: The first reference to a church at Broadfield was in 1220 when a rector was presented to Rushden church and was forbidden to interfere with the chapel at Broadfield. Apparently, it had been quit-claimed by the lord of Rushden shortly before then. Two years later, however, Broadfield was referred to as a rectory with the advowson held by the manor. So it remained, at least until 1346. After that date there was no mention of the church until the ecclesiastical investigation of Edward VI; in 1535 Broadfield was worth 10 s. per annum. Though still considered a rectory, it was extremely poor - the poorest place in the Lincoln Diocese of Hertfordshire, poorer than small chapels and chantries. Rushden, which since 1336 had been a priory, was almost twenty times as wealthy. It would be unimaginable for anyone to have made his living from the Broadfield benefice. In 1518 and in 1530, Broadfield was not mentioned in the episcopal visitations to Hertfordshire. Neither was it mentioned in the inventory of 1553, though the advowson was still included in a late sixteenth century sale of the manor. John Norden wrote in 1598 that at Broadfield there was "a chapel of ease now decayed" [Norden 1903, 12]. It had been, of course, a rectory since 1222 at least, though Norden would not have recognized it from the 'decay'. By the eighteenth century Broadfield was ecclesiastically attached to Cottered, and it may have been also in Norden's time, letting him assume it to have been a chapel of ease, perhaps Cottered. At least, in 1636, documentary evidence attested to its extinction; Broadfield was referred to as "sine clerici" (see Appendix B).

THE VILLAGE: The only description of the village at Broadfield was that in the Domesday Book. Here the estate totals (for all four holdings) were 4 villiens, 5 bordars, 3 serfs, and 2 cottars, as well as land for almost 4 plough teams, plenty of pasture, and woodland for 90 swine. There were fourteen tenants in all, and using a factor of 3.5 (family per tenant), the population would have been about fifty persons. By 1300 there may have been around one hundred inhabitants, but the small size of the parish would make that a maximum.

The remaining documentary evidence comes from taxes. The fourteenth century tax was 26s. 3d. [Beresford 1969, 356], fairly low for the

region, and in 1446 Broadfield's tax relief was 64% [Beresford 1969, 356].
While these figures were perhaps arbitary, they do show a general decline
of the village. The Subsidy Roll of 1545 has only two Broadfield tax-
payers, each paying only 2d. [Brigg 1895, 352]. It was the poorest parish
in the hundred. Certainly, by that time, the village, as such, was non-
existant.

Broadfield Hall was begun c. 1650 [Hine 1951, 4] and rebuilt in the
nineteenth century. An earlier hall was not mentioned in any documents, nor
by Norden [Norden 1903, 15]. However, one must assume that there was a
medieval manor on the site, if only from the 1690 expense of "filling in the
old moat" [Hine 1951, 6].

IV. TOPOGRAPHY OF THE VILLAGE

Broadfield Parish (374 acres) is triangular in shape, the eastern side
lying along the crest of a low ridge (Fig. 1). The other two sides descend
westward from that ridge along natural water courses. Most of the land is
arable, with three small woods lying north of the manor and village site. It
is well watered, but not protected from the wind. The average altitude is
450 ft. above sea level; it lies well above the surrounding countryside.

The village site has been photographed from the air by the R. A. F.
(No. 3074 9-JAN 47 F/L 20// 58 SQDN) and by Dr. J. K. St. Joseph, Director
of Aerial Photography at the University of Cambridge (147/325311). These
photographs show indistinct features, many of which are post-medieval in
origin. It is by the synthesis of aerial photography and ground observation
that a village topography can tentatively be put forward (Fig. 2).

There are several probable hollow ways as well as croft sites.
However, much of the village appears to have been destroyed by the manor
and its farm buildings. Continuity of boundary is evident in two places. The
south edge of the Great Wood is in alignment with the main east-west
hollow way. To the west, the north-south earthwork is on the line of the
present east boundary of field No. 4 (Fig. 1). Fields Nos. 1-5 also show

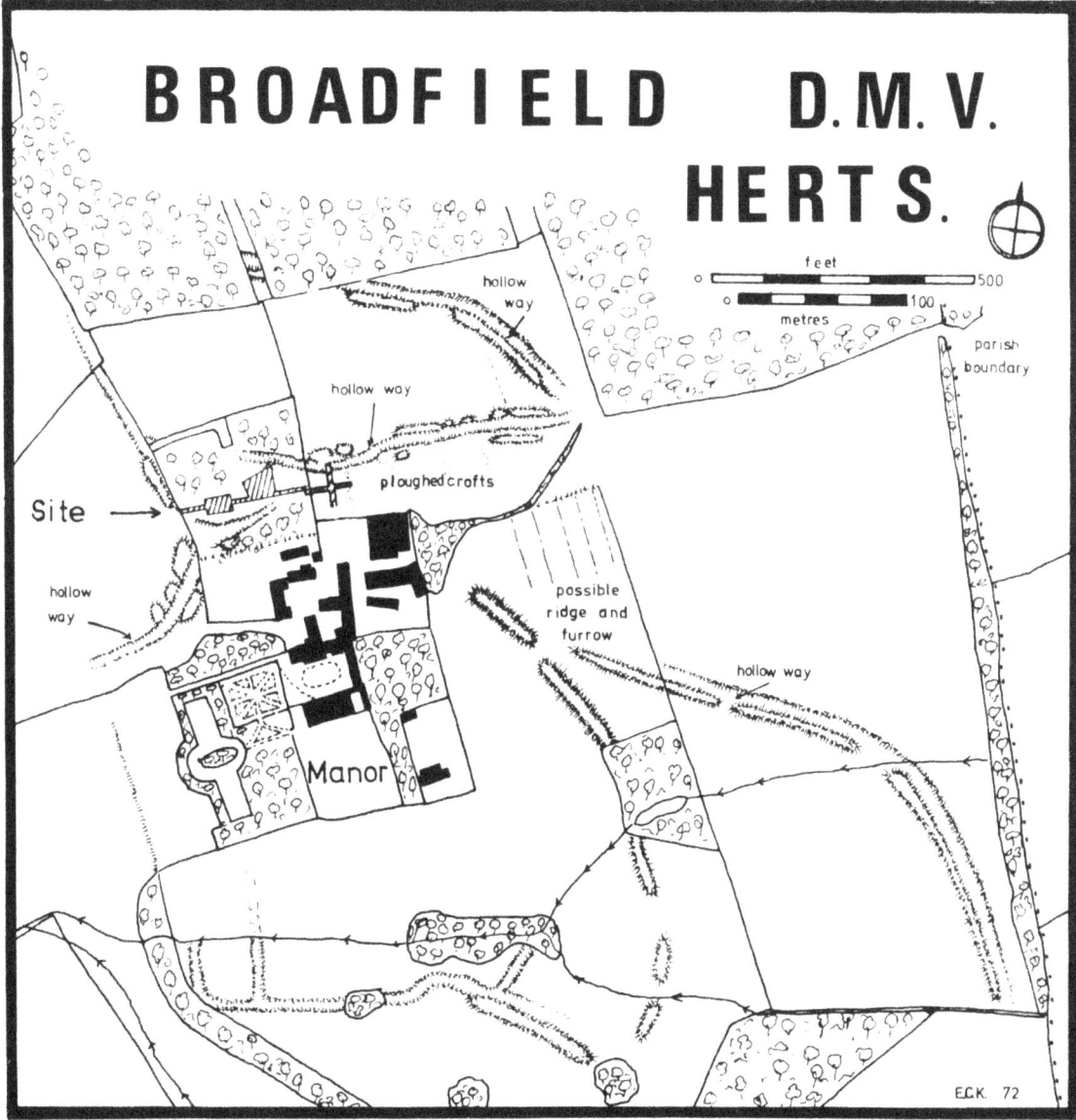

BROADFIELD D.M.V.
HERTS.

feet
500

metres
100

parish boundary

hollow way

hollow way

ploughed crofts

Site

hollow way

possible ridge and furrow

hollow way

Manor

E.C.K. 72

Fig. 2

7

the familiar medieval 'reversed - S' curve of ridge and furrow. Fields Nos. 6-8 may show this pattern to a lesser degree.

V. THE EXCAVATIONS (Fig. 3)

TECHNIQUES: The platform shown on the east side of Fig. 3 was cross-trenched and partly stripped (B and C). The central enclosure and western platform were explored by a single 4' trench, 250' long, from east to west (D-M). In the western enclosure this was expanded to an open area of 970 sq. ft. (O and N). The church site was an open area of 3,820 sq. ft., with exploratory trenches southward to establish the limit of the cemetery. The major east-west trenches of the first excavation could not be coterminous because of the orchard trees.

SUMMARY:

> Period I. Pre-church features - peasant timber buildings and boundary ditches. c.1100 - c.1220.

> Period II. Church and associated features - two-phased church and its enclosure ditches, contemporary peasant occupation. c.1220 - c.1450.

> Period III. Post-church features - drainage ditches and agricultural levelling. c.1450 - 1965.

GENERAL STRATIFICATION:

> I Pre-church features. The early features were cut into the natural boulder clay and were associated with a brown occupation deposit. None were visible from the surface, and most had been cut by later features, especially in the cemetery.

> II Church and associated features. Little was visible on the surface in the church area, though the features there were generally well defined and exhibited the same alignment. The features of the western platform were poorly defined and badly disturbed by later features.

> III Post-church features. Most of these features were visible on

8

BROADFIELD D.M.V.

Site Plan ; 1965

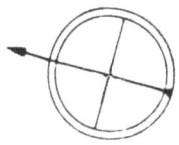

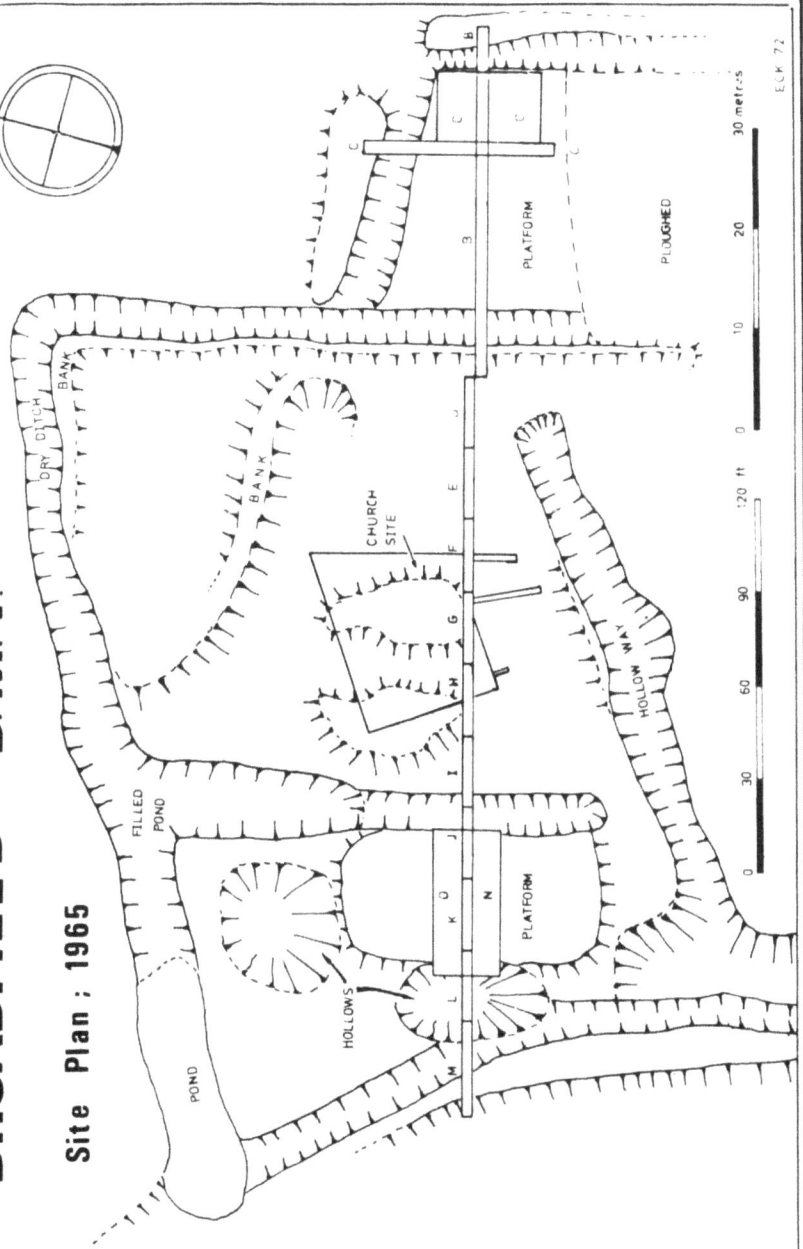

CHURCH SITE

DRY DITCH

BANK

BANK

FILLED POND

POND

HOLLOWS

PLATFORM

PLATFORM

HOLLOW WAY

PLOUGHED

ECK 72

30 metres

120 ft

Fig. 3

the surface. Most cut through earlier features, and there were several instances of superimposition of ditches. The numerous modern land-drains (marked L. D. on the plans) confused the stratification in places.

For all periods, in all areas, the recording of stratification and the measurements of features were limited, occasionally insufficient. This was due to the nature of the rescue work and to the high water table throughout the site. Except for the church site, the names given to the features and to the layers filling them were not differentiated by the excavators. In the instances where no measurements are given for features, this is because no measurements were recorded.

TRENCHES : EAST PLATFORM (Fig. 4)

General Description. The two trenches (B and C) were exploratory, each 4' wide. The open area C was to confirm the findings of trenches B and C, namely that the 'platform' was merely an area defined by the cutting of post-medieval drainage ditches.

Trench B. At the east end of the trench, the platform ditch was sectioned, revealing extensive post-medieval recutting and a possible late medieval ditch of dark silt which contained no finds. Through the platform, no features were found, except modern tractor marks and post-medieval debris.

To the west a linear depression was found with a fill of yellow silt, B20, below a brown soil, B10. This was in a line with the visible hollow way cutting obliquely through the trench and having a width of c. 6'. Appearing on the surface of B20, but sealed by B10, were F.1, F.2, and F.4. All were post holes. F.1 was triangular and contained three post sockets, each 9" in diameter, 6" deep. F.2 was a circular post socket with the charcoal remains of a burnt post in situ, 9" in diameter, 18" deep, and pointed at the end. F.4 was 9" square, and also 18" deep; no post socket was discernable.

In the west end of trench B, the east churchyard boundary ditch was sectioned, revealing a post-medieval ditch (A) cutting a medieval ditch (B). The latter was not observable on the surface, as it had been partially cut by

10

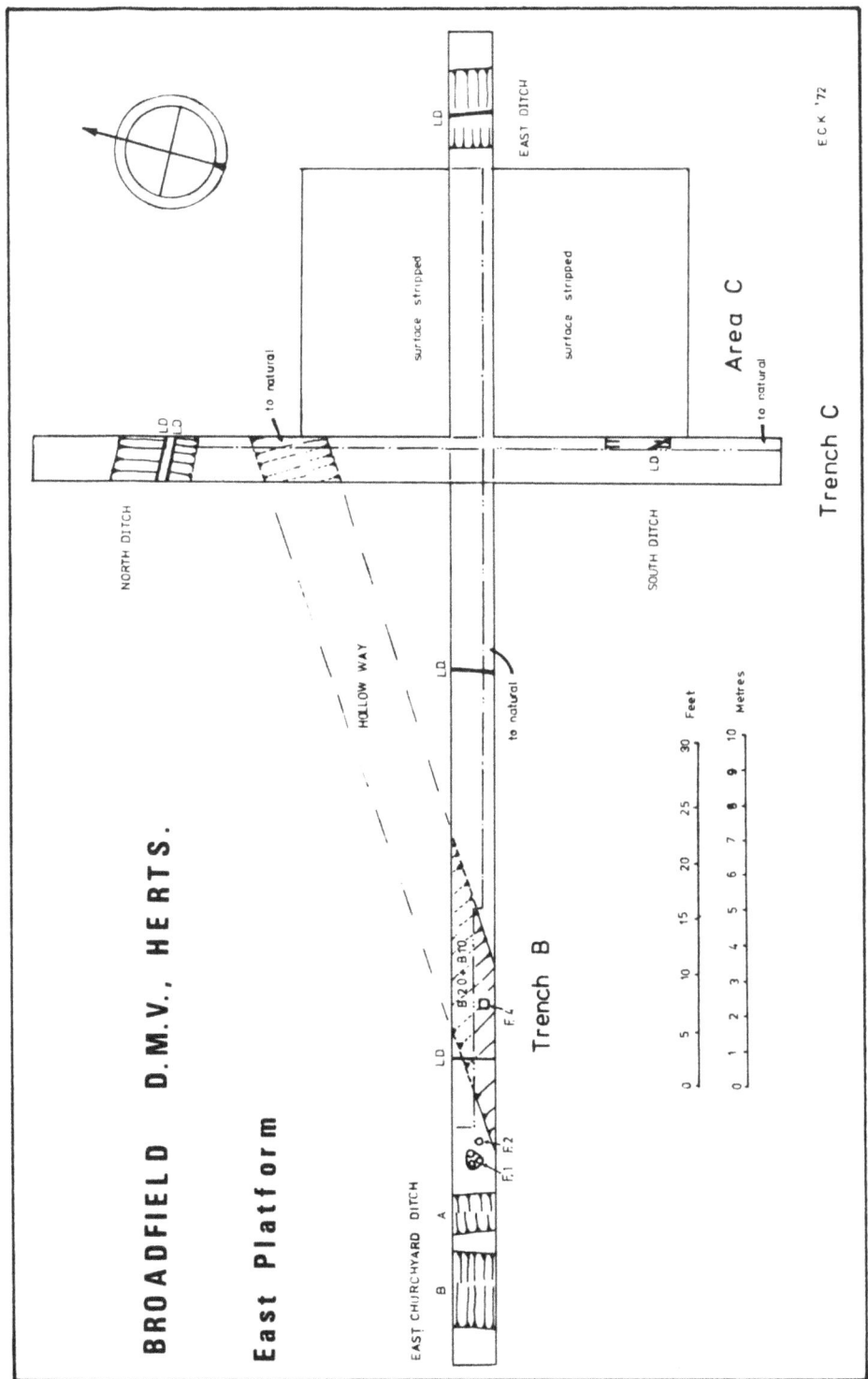

BROADFIELD D.M.V., HERTS.

East Platform

EAST CHURCHYARD DITCH

NORTH DITCH

HOLLOW WAY

Trench B

B20 B70
F4
F1 F2

LD

to natural

surface stripped

surface stripped

EAST DITCH

LD

SOUTH DITCH

LD

to natural

Area C

to natural

Trench C

ECK '72

Feet   Metres

0   5   10   15   20   25   30

0   1   2   3   4   5   6   7   8   9   10

Fig. 4

the later ditch and partially sealed by its spoil. Ditch A was presumably a drainage ditch, as it had been recut several times, and even carried a modern land drain. It followed the line of the medieval ditch which presumably was a boundary ditch only, as it had not been substantially recut. In the absence of other evidence, the medieval ditch can be assigned to the establishment of the church and churchyard in the early thirteenth century.

Trench C. A feature 6' wide and 1' deep was found in the southern end of trench C. This shallow ditch was of post-medieval construction as its spoil lay upon a layer containing post-medieval debris. It was perhaps a drainage ditch, augmenting those to the east and west. No angle could be ascertained. No features could be found on the rest of the platform, and the only occupation spread was post-medieval.

Cutting obliguely through the north part of trench C, the hollow way was sectioned and was found to be c. 8' wide with a fill of yellow silt. Its upper levels were filled with a dark soil, and presumably the hollow way had been deliberately levelled for agricultural activity.

In the extreme north of trench C, a ditch was sectioned. This ditch was observable on the surface and was not completely excavated as it was badly disturbed by modern drainage ditches and land drains which followed the line of the earlier ditch. In its later stages, it certainly was a drainage ditch; its fill had far more humus than that of the hollow way crossing trenches B and C.

Area C. No features were recorded in area C. However, a post-medieval spread of debris through the centre of the platform was uncovered.

TRENCHES : CENTRAL ENCLOSURE (Figs. 3, 9)

General Description. It was an exploratory trench, 4' wide, crossing the central enclosure from east to west, south of the church. Each section of the trench was 24' long. The general stratigraphy was turf and topsoil to 9", lower topsoil or rubble to 12", buff clayey soil to 24", and natural.

Trenches D, E, F. No features were revealed in these areas.

Trench G. A rubble layer of mortar and tile fragments, G4, was uncovered below the topsoil. It began ten feet from the east end of trench G and continued west. Beneath it were located several graves at different levels, and three post holes. All were in a dark buff clayey layer, G5. Any earlier features were destroyed by the graves, several of which were dug into natural.

Trench H. In trench H the rubble layer, H4, continued westward ending three feet from the west end of H. Beneath it was a dark buff clayey layer and below that, a layer of flint cobbling and several graves in a buff clayey soil. The deposit of the buff clayey soil above the cobbling, H5, can be ascribed to grave digging. Two post holes were located among the graves.

TRENCHES : WEST PLATFORM (Fig. 5)

General Description. The 4' wide exploratory trench was continued westward; each section was 24' long except M which was 32' long. Areas N and O, south and north, respectively, of the trench were opened up. Each was 10' by 48'6". The general stratigraphy was topsoil and lower topsoil to 12", cobbles or occupation layer to 15", light buff clayey soil to 24", and natural.

Trench I. There were no features in I except those shared with J.

Trench J. (Fig. 6) In the east of J, the west churchyard enclosure ditch was sectioned. It revealed a ditch silted in grey brown chalky soil, J4a, which was sealed by an infill of chalky clay, J4, over this. J4 continued westward as a spread below the lower topsoil and contained many tile fragments. In the silted fill, J4a, there was a single piece of tile.

To the east of the ditch, and cut by it, there was found a north-south beam slot with a charcoal stained fill, J7. To the west of the ditch, an east-west beam slot was located, with a dark, charcoal flecked fill, J6, and some daub fragments. A portion of this extended a little way to the east of J7. The actual cutting of these features by the ditch was covered by a slipping of buff clayey soil, J5a, on either side of the ditch. The buff clayey soil J5 covered the beam slot J6 to the west of the ditch. Below the east-west beam slot J6 was found a feature, the northern terminus of a north-south beam slot, parallel to J7, with a fill of charcoal and daub fragments, J6a.

Trench K. A cobbled surface appeared below a layer of buff clay, K5, below the lower topsoil. It began in the centre of the cutting and continued westward.

Trench L. In the east end of L, the earth sloped down to the west; the cobbled surface from trench K stopped 8' past the east end. From there to 3' from the east end of M, there were extensive ditch recuttings filled with a homogeneous black silt, L3, L4, L5. Below this was the cutting of the original north-south Ditch 1, c. 5' wide. Its upper fill, L6, was dark grey. Its bottom was not excavated. Three feet from the west end, the trench was cut by a modern land drain. East of this and continuing into trench M was found another north-south ditch, Ditch 2, c. 4' wide. This was cut into buff clayey soil and sealed by a spread of flints and chalk below the topsoil.

Trench M. A single layer of disturbed rubble was recorded, with divisions from east to west, 3a - 3d. The remainder of Ditch 2 continued, sealed by a spread of flints and chalk, M3a. After a slight rise of 6", M3b sealed Ditch 3, only 1' deep and 6' wide, filled with brown clayey soil, M10. M3b had several tile fragments among chalk lumps. A post hole, M7, with a diameter of 9", was found in M3b. West of Ditch 3, M3c continued on the same level as M3a and M3b but had more brown soil and less chalk. Eighteen feet from the east end of trench M, portions of an oven or hearth were found, burnt clay and charcoal, M8. At forty feet from the east end of trench M. the platform ended in a 45 degree slope, with much evidence of erosion. Before the edge, layer M3d was a deeper brown and contained little chalk.

Area N. South of trenches J, K, L, an area 10' by 48'6" was opened up. In the east part of N, the western edge of the churchyard ditch was followed southward. The same silt and chalky fill and spread, N6, were found here as in trench J. To the west of this, there was found a north-south beam slot (in J, J6a) with a dirty brown fill, N8. A curving east-west feature was located in the central eastern area of N. Its fill was very dark soil, N11. West of this was located an area of burnt clay, N7, roughly circular, 2' in diameter. This hearth area was compact, but had a slight extension to the

BROADFIELD D.M.V., HERTS.

West Platform

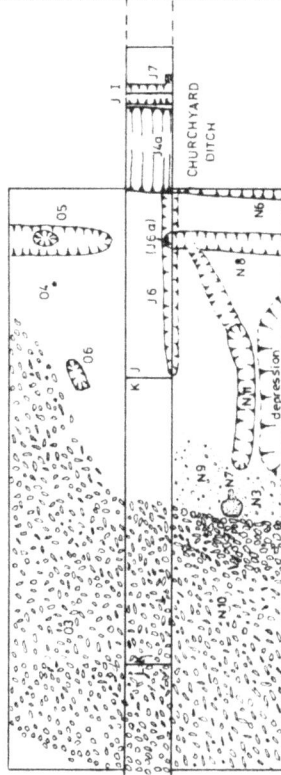

Platform Edge

Ditch, Beam Slot, or Post Hole

Cobbling

Hearth

Mortar Rubble

0   5   10   15   20   25   30 Feet

0   1   2   3   4   5   6   7   8   9   10 Metres

ECK '72

Fig. 5

SECTION OF CHURCHYARD DITCH; TRENCH J

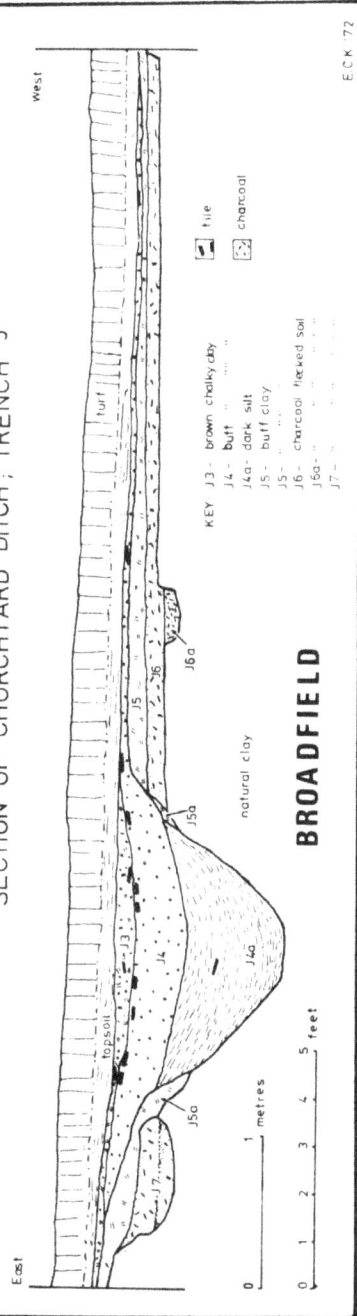

KEY J3 - brown chalky clay
J4 - buff
J4a - dark silt
J5 - buff clay
J5a -
J6 - charcoal flecked soil
J6a -
J7 -

tile

charcoal

natural clay

topsoil

turf

West

East

BROADFIELD

0   1   2   3   4   5 feet

0   1 metres

ECK '72

Fig. 6

east.

Above all these features was a layer of flints with tile fragments, N5, over which was laid the chalk spread, N2 - N6, in which were found fragments of quern and a piece of carved stone - a coffin lid - Worked Stone 1. Associated with these features and sealed by N5 were areas of mortar, stone, and burnt clay, N3 and N9. These ended at the west end of the hearth, N7, and were replaced by a thick, compact layer of cobbling, N10, with a definite eastern edge. This cobbling continued west through area N.

Area O. North of trenches J, K, L, an area 10' by 48'6" was opened up. In the east of O, a north-south feature, O5, 2'6" wide, was located. In its northern part, a deeper area (2' by 3') was found. The fill was dark, charcoal flecked soil. It was not well recorded and appeared to have been two features, a beam slot cut by a post hole. Three feet west of O5 was a stake hole, O4, 3" in diameter and 8" into the natural. Further west was a post hole, O6, 3' by 2', and badly disturbed. To the west, an ill defined northeast-southwest edge of cobbles was found. This cobbling spread over the western part of area O, except the extreme northwest.

THE CHURCH SITE

General Description. An area of 3,820 sq. ft. was opened up, north of the central east-west trench. The interior of the church was excavated to buried soil beneath the church construction levels. Outside, most areas were taken down to natural. The cemetery was excavated primarily at its northern edge. Later, however, it was trenched to discover the layout of the graves. Several exploratory trenches were also dug south of the site, to establish the limits of the cemetery (Fig. 3).

Church Stratigraphy. (Fig. 7) 1. Turf and topsoil. 2. Lower topsoil. 3. Rubble outside walls. 4. Rubble inside walls, with a charcoal base. 5. Sterile clay deposit. 6. Mortar spread north of church. 7. Rubble spread east of church. 8. Mixed clayey soil outside church. 9. Dark mortary soil with flint and tile fragments in chancel. 10. Thick yellow mortar deposit in chancel. 11. Yellow mortar spread in nave with base of dark soil. 12. Subfloor level of clunch and mortar. 13. Red brown soil with mortar bits.

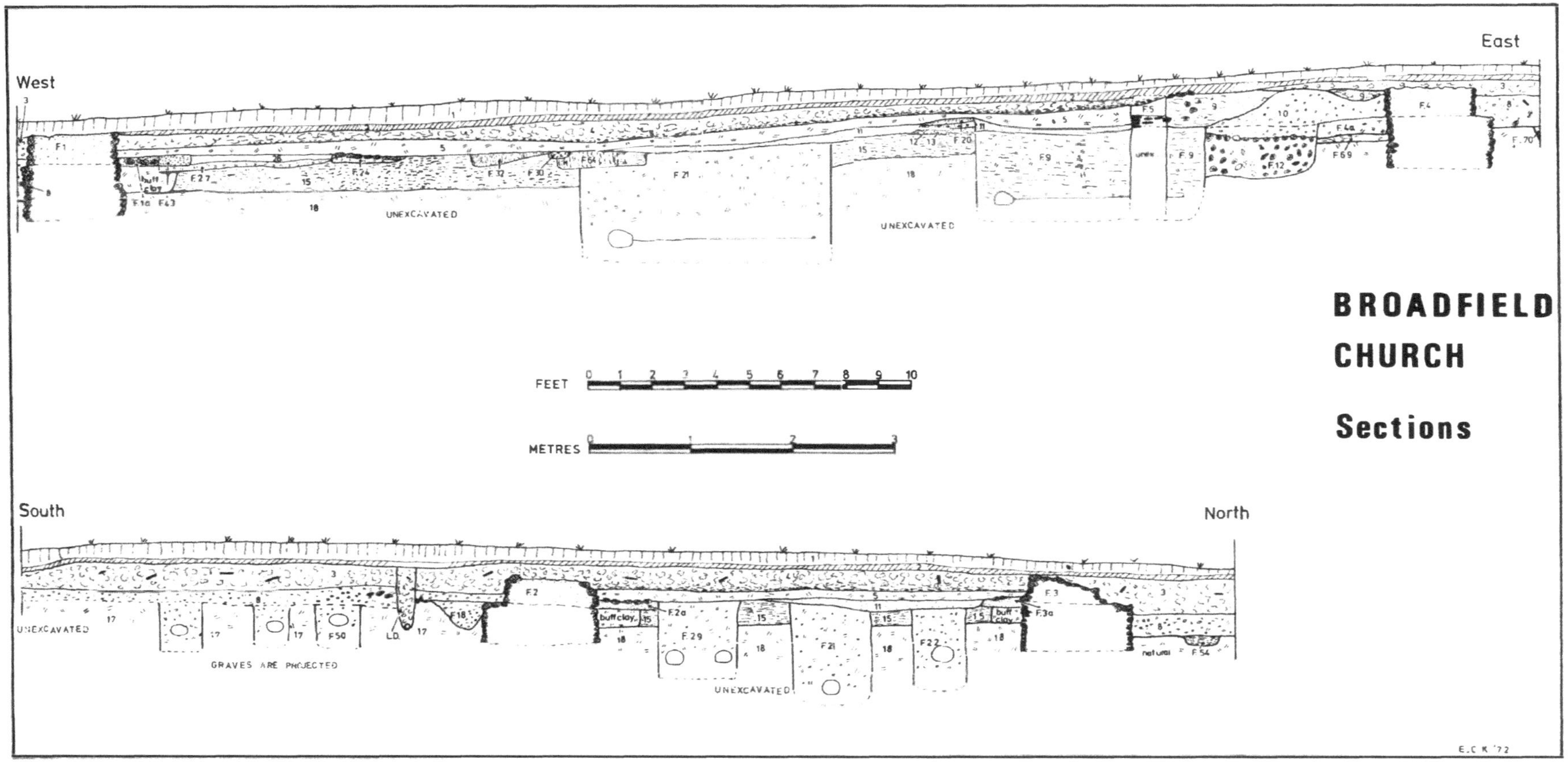

BROADFIELD CHURCH Sections

Fig. 7

Please note that a full-size version of this figure is available to download from www.barpublishing.com/additional-downloads.html

The original foldout has been reduced in size to match the A4 format of this book, the image is therefore not as clear as the original foldout. Please refer to the original foldout via the download for the original content.

14. Patchy mortary soil with chalk and clunch in west nave. 15. Buried soil, dark grey with heavy charcoal flecking. 16. Dark charcoal flecked soil in cemetery. 17. Disturbed clayey soil with chalk nodules in cemetery. 18. Charcoal flecked red brown clay, disturbed natural.

PRE-CHURCH FEATURES : PERIOD I (Fig. 8)

Features 42, 72, 68, 15, and 16 were segments of a north-south ditch, c. 2' wide, cut by the wall foundations and disappearing in the cemetery. Its fill was dark ashy soil containing no mortar. Running east-west was F.57, a small drainage ditch, sealed by the cemetery cobbling, F.31.

Outside the church were several other early features. F.52 was a beam slot cut by the south nave wall; F.56 was a small post hole; and F.55 was a drain or sump filled with sherds and animal bones. To the north were F.53, a post hole, and F.54, a sump the channel to which was badly disturbed by tree roots. Both were sealed by layer 8.

Inside the nave, in layer 15 were F.49 a pit cut by the north nave wall, F.34 a small post hole cut by F.27, and F.33 a post hole cut by the south nave wall. In the chancel was F.71 cut into layer 15. F.69 appeared to be part of an east-west ditch joining F.72 with F.45. Its fill was dark soil with sherds and bones and cut 1' into the natural.

South of the chancel was F.19, a small post hole just outside the cemetery. To the east were F.70 a post hole sealed by layer 8, F.47 a pit disturbed by a later pit F.10, and F.45 the western edge of a north-south ditch, disturbed by graves. F.73 was a flint cobble spread with indefinite edges, continuing past the limit of excavation.

Other pre-church features were several sets of post holes inside the nave. F.51 was a double post hole with mortar in the top of its fill. F.58 and F.59 had upper fills of red clay, but lower down had fills of mortary soil. These three features had been cut by infant burials, and their upper levels had been removed or disturbed. Features 35, 36, 37, 38 had the same fill, yellow mortar. F.36 was cut by grave feature 21, and F.35 was sealed by flint and mortar packing F.3a. F.39 was an isolated stake hole; it had the same mortar fill as the others. Although their measurements were not recorded, the similarity of fill and nature of these features would separate them from the other pre-church features, and put them in a sub-phase, Period Ib.

CHURCH FEATURES : PERIOD II (Figs. 7, 9)

Walls. The walls, Features 1 - 4, were aligned east-west. Their dimensions were for the west wall, F. 1, exterior length 19' 2", interior length 13' 10", width 2' 10"; for the south wall, F. 2, exterior length 44' 9", interior length 39' $9\frac{1}{2}$", width 2' 10"; for the north wall, F. 3, exterior length 44' 8". interior length 39' $7\frac{1}{2}$", width 2' 9"; for the east wall, F. 4, exterior length 19' 2", interior length 13' 7", width 2' 8", slightly narrower than the other walls.

The north door, F. 3c, was 3' wide; the south door, F. 2c, was less well preserved, but would have been about the same width. Three feet west of F. 4 was the robbed foundation of a north-south wall, F. 12. Its dimensions, as well as could be ascertained, were the same as the west wall, F. 1. (see Appendix D for comparison with Throcking Church)

Construction. The wall footings were made of flint with brown chalky soil and were put into almost vertical wall trenches. The church walls were also of flint, but had yellow mortar, and were not aligned directly on top of the footings. Perhaps the church was slightly realigned after the foundations had been built. Dressed sandstone was used at the corners. The primary east wall, F. 12, was robbed to its foundations, but apparently the external corners were not robbed as the new extensions were straight jointed. The dressed stone was removed from the original corners and perhaps reused in those of the secondary east wall.

Interior Foundations. Running along the wall edges and cutting into the buried soil, layer 15, were foundation trenches filled with sterile buff clay. These were not given feature numbers, except for F. 4a, the inner foundation trench for the secondary east wall (F. 4). Lying above these cuttings, but overlapping and cutting into their upper fill as well as into layer 15, were F. 1a, F. 2a, F. 3a, mortar and flint packing 4" thick. These areas of packing were generally 2' wide and ran parallel to the walls. They were

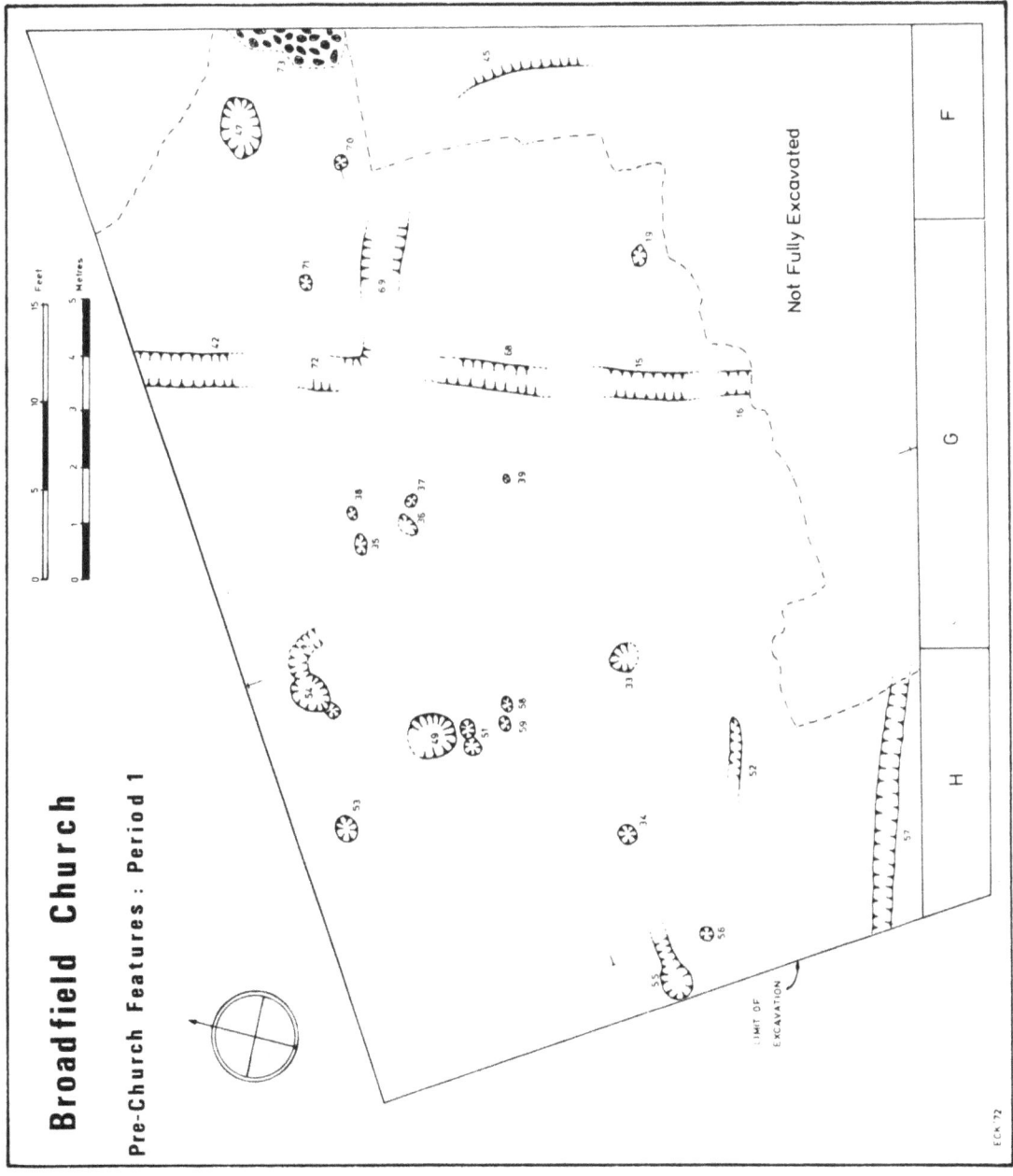

Broadfield Church

Pre-Church Features : Period 1

15 Feet

5 Metres

Not Fully Excavated

F

G

H

LIMIT OF
EXCAVATION

ECK '72

Fig. 8

interrupted at the north and south doorways and ended easterly at the chancel steps. Two later features appear to be additions to the packing. F. 43 was an expansion in the northwest corner of the nave, 12" wide and cut into layer 15, 2" deep. F. 11 in the southeast corner of the nave extended 6" to 24" into the nave, and was irregular in shape. F. 11 also resurfaced the original F. 2a, but did not extend further to the east.

Interior Features. Six feet from the secondary east wall and parallel to it was a sanctuary step, F. 5, height 9", width 1' 1". It was made of clunch blocks with a foundation of mortared tile courses. The top stones were worn on the surface and western edge. The step was not placed exactly centrally, the distance from the north wall being 2' and from the south wall being 2' 7". It may have been aligned with the east grave (F. 9), which was equally off centre.

In the east part of the nave, a floor level of grey clunch and mortar, F. 20, was preserved. It was cut by the east grave (F. 9) and sealed by the mortar spread of layer 11. Upon F. 20 was a burnt area, F. 17, located in the northeast corner of the nave. The west end of the nave contained several features. F. 24 was a font soak-away of hard grey clay with tiles, flints, and chalk nodules. Cut by F. 24 was an area of grey clay, F. 27, abutting F. 1a. This deposit was the fill of a depression, a previous font soak-away.

Exterior Features. Directly outside the south doorway was a raised area of gravel and mortar, F. 48. This exterior threshold marks a break in F. 18, which was a channel filled with brown silt. It ran at a slight angle to the south wall. Further east, F. 46 appeared to be a continuation of F. 18. It may have been a pathway to the south doorway, though at the north doorway there were no such features. Southwest of the church was an area of flint cobbling, F. 31. This cobbling extended southeast to trench K. Containing few sherds and sealing the pre-church layer 16, it was itself cut by several graves.

Interior Graves. Inside the church appeared eight graves, two of which were double burials. All were orientated along the axis of the church, with heads to the west. F. 9 lay beneath the chancel steps and abutted the

Broadfield Church

Church Features : Period 2

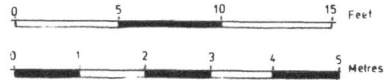

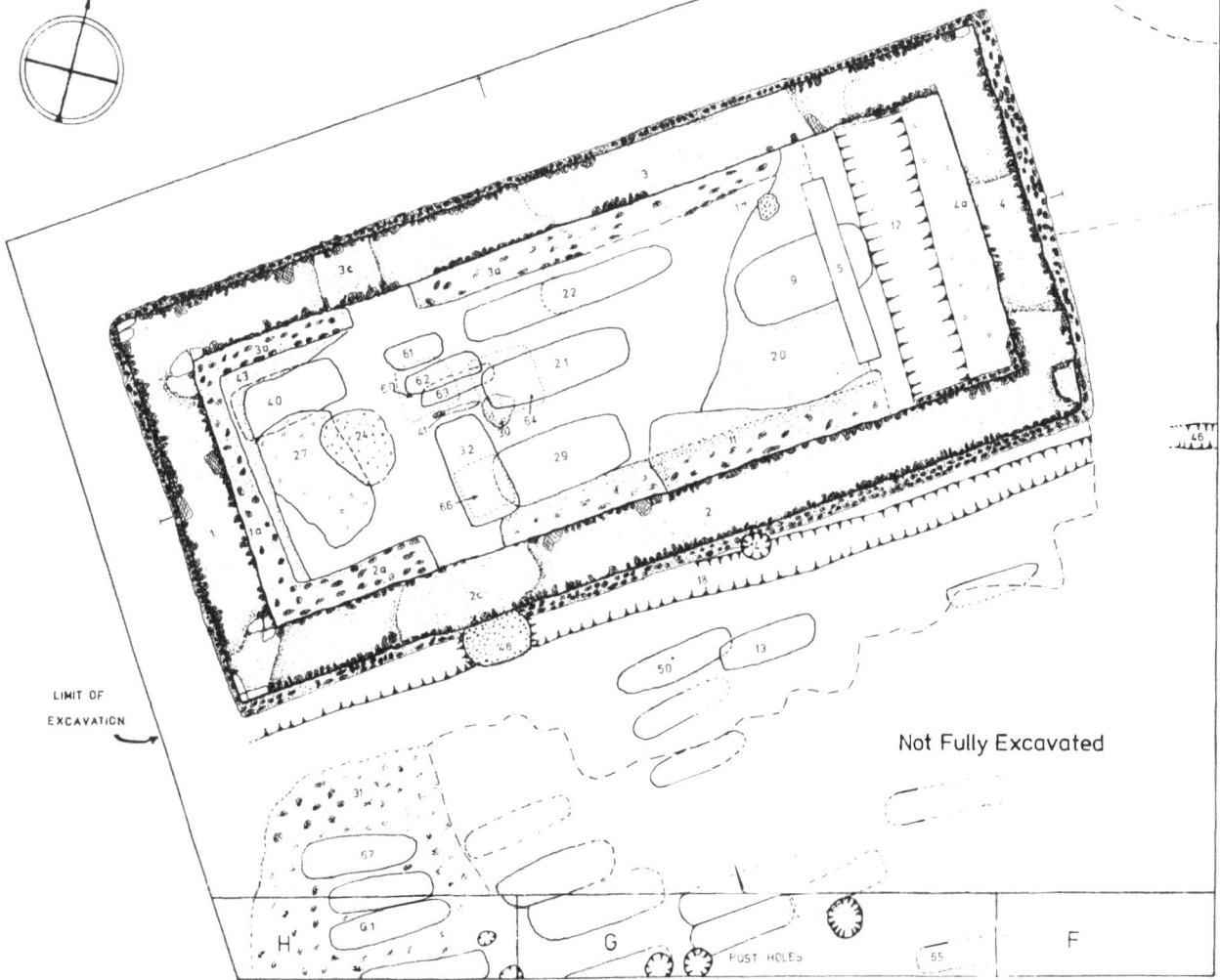

Not Fully Excavated

LIMIT OF
EXCAVATION

POST HOLES

H   G   F

ECK 72

Fig. 9

Please note that a full-size version of this figure is available to download from
www.barpublishing.com/additional-downloads.html

The original foldout has been reduced in size to match the A4 format of this book, the image is therefore not as
clear as the original foldout. Please refer to the original foldout via the download for the original content.

primary east wall foundation. It measured 7' long, 3' wide, 4' deep, and contained a single skeleton. The fill was dark, mortary soil.

Of the three central graves, the most northerly, F.22, was actually two graves intersecting on their axis, the easternmost being the secondary. Each contained a single skeleton and measured 2' wide and c.6' 6" long. The secondary skull was found at a depth of 3'. The fill of both was red clay. The middle grave, F.21, was a single burial, again with a red clay fill. It was less than 3' wide and over 7' long; the skull was found at a depth of 5'. The southern grave, F.29, contained a male and a female skeleton, as well as a child's skull at a higher level. The male skeleton was primary, with the female above it. Associated with the female burial were heavy coffin stains and many coffin nails in the fill. The depths of the skulls were about 3' and 4'; the fill was red clay.

In the northwest corner of the nave, F.40 was found, a red clay filled pit with vertical sides, 5' 6" long and 2' 6" wide. Although it was orientated to the church axis, it contained no skeleton. It may have been an infant's burial (perhaps multiple), the bones of which had disintegrated. Three infant burials were found, however, to the east of the north doorway. The most northerly was F.61, measuring 3' long, 1' 6" wide, 3' deep. Its fill was brown soil, not red clay. The middle grave, F.62, had the red clay fill, and was 4' long, 1' 6" wide, c.3' deep. It contained a scrap of bronze (Bronze No. 3) and cut F.63, the most southerly of the infant burials. F.63 itself was badly disturbed by F.62, and both graves were cut by F.21. The dimensions of F.63 were c.4' long, c.1' 6" wide, 3' deep; its fill was the common red clay.

Memorial Slab Cuttings. There were three shallow square cuttings over graves, presumably for memorial slabs. F.60 covered the heads of the infant burials, F.62 and F.63. It had a fill of red clay; its depth was 3", and each side was c.3' long. F.64 had the same dimensions as F.60 and covered the head of grave F.21. Its fill was brown chalky soil. F.66 was the same type feature, over the heads in grave F.29, but its dimensions were difficult to define as it had been badly disturbed by F.32.

Opposite : Plates Ia and Ib.

22

F. 32 was a shallow north-south cutting, deeper to the west. It cut into F. 29 and disturbed most of F. 66; it may have been dug to remove the memorial slab in F. 66. To the north of F. 32 were F. 30 and F. 41, areas of burning, the latter of which was filled with grey clunch. Their exact stratigraphical position was not recorded, but they appeared to be associated with F. 32 and a period of disturbance to the church interior.

Exterior Graves. Several graves were identified in the cemetery, but the height of the water table prevented further investigation. Only Grave 1 was excavated fully; it lay in trench H. Its dimensions were recorded as 5' 5" long, 1' 6" wide, 2' 7" depth to skull; its fill was reddish brown clay. (See Section VIII, Part 11). Other graves of the cemetery were F. 16, F. 65, F. 50, and F. 67, the last of which may have been re-covered with flint cobbling. F. 14 was an infant burial against the south wall of the church. It was late, and possibly post-church, as it cut into the silt of F. 18, the path to the south doorway.

POST-CHURCH FEATURES : PERIOD III (Not Illustrated)

The destruction levels contained few features. East of the church, a pit was found, F. 10, which cut into the top of earlier F. 47. F. 10 contained much burnt debris, including stained glass fragments and pieces of window lead. By the northeast corner of the church was a rubble deposit, F. 28, which may have been the result of the reuse of stones from the church. Inside the building a depression filled with mortary brown soil cut across the rubble over the south wall. This possible footpath ignored the alignment of the church. Two other features appeared in the rubble spread. A dog burial, F. 6, had been re-covered by rubble, and a lamb burial, F. 7, was more recent as it was not covered by the rubble, but by the topsoil.

VI. INTERPRETATION

EAST PLATFORM

The east platform was not a house platform but the result of post-medieval drainage cuttings. These earthworks also sealed part of the hollow way going through the area southwest to northeast. In the silted hollow way, but below the post-medieval deliberate filling, were post holes, perhaps part of an enclosure. Their construction ignored the hollow way and were dug after village life had declined.

The line of the east churchyard ditch was retained and recut for drainage purposes in the post-medieval period. North of the 'platform', an east-west ditch had been recut many times. However, its original wide, shallow shape precludes its use for drainage. Most likely, it was a hollow way which was turned into a boundary and drainage ditch. This hollow way would have been replaced by the one to the south, running northeast to southwest. The northern way was used in Period I, and the southern way replaced it in Period II. By Period III, the southern way was silted up, and in that period it was filled and levelled, and the area became the agricultural 'platform'.

WEST PLATFORM (Fig. 10)

Period I. In the eastern part of the west platform there was a house orientated north-south. Its construction was of sill beams with some use of post holes. The angles of the walls were invariably 90 degrees, with only slight deviations. No floor level remained, and the total dimensions were not discovered. At one point, at least, it was 25' wide, though this may represent the attachment of an ancillary room. The main north-south bay was almost 15' wide and was at least 24' long (the limits of the excavation). This building seems so well constructed that it may have been the pre-church manor.

Period II. Through the centre of the sill beamed building was cut the west churchyard ditch, at a slight angle to the previous orientation. To the west, a new building was constructed. Its dimensions could not be clearly

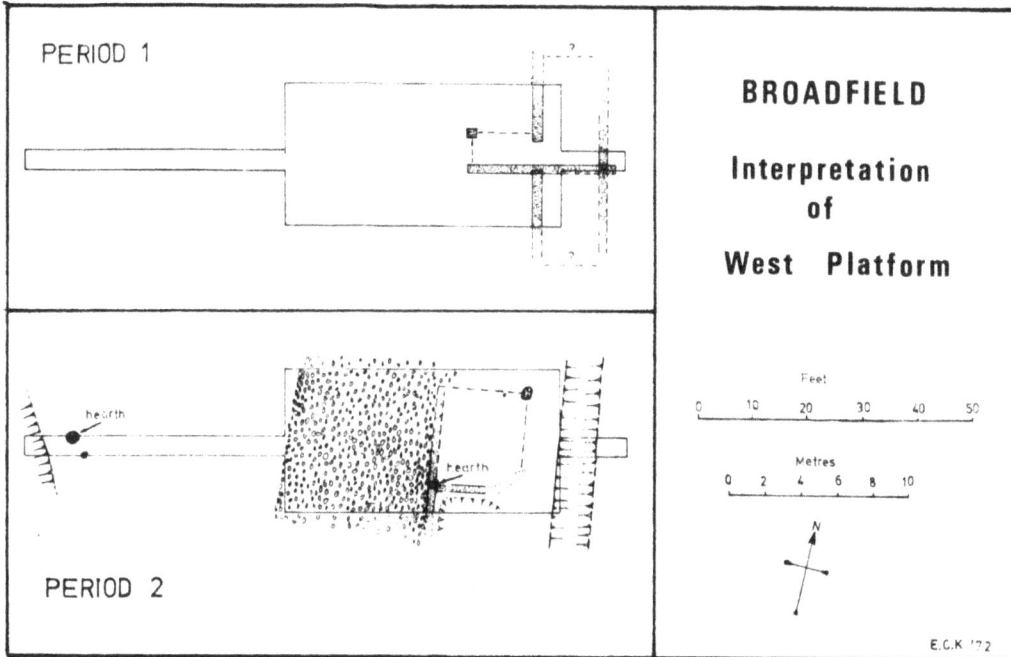

PERIOD 1

PERIOD 2

hearth

hearth

BROADFIELD

Interpretation
of

West Platform

Feet
0   10   20   30   40   50

Metres
0   2   4   6   8   10

N

E.C.K '72

Fig. 10

defined, but along part of its western wall there remained a sharp edge of cobbling. It may have been c. 15' wide and more than 22' long, and of mixed construction. From the amount of mortar and rubble, the west wall may have been, like the church, of flint and mortar. The other walls were presumably of a post hole and raised beam construction, though there is some doubt as to the compatibility of two such different building techniques and to the reason for their combined use. Also, there was one beam slot which curiously curved and faded away, adding further to the irregular structure of the building.

At the join of the beam slot wall and the west wall, there was a corner oven, not uncommon in medieval houses. On the south side of the internal cross-wall there was a depression which may have marked a different function for this southern area, though domestic buildings of this period often had depressed floor levels, attributed to constant sweeping. The orientation of both the house and its cobbled yard was parallel to the churchyard ditch.

At the extreme west of the trench, there was another building of which only a hearth and one post hole were discovered. Thus, its dimensions, construction, and orientation are not known. As it was beside the edge of the platform, the erosion of that bank may have destroyed some portions of the building.

Period III. The churchyard ditch, having silted extensively, was filled in with chalky soil, which was also spread over much of this area. Its line was not retained, as was that of the east churchyard ditch. No further occupation took place, though the area was used for agricultural purposes in the post-medieval period. Three ditches were cut obliquely northwest-southeast through the site and ran through what must have been the area of the western building. Later agricultural activity spread rubble from the earlier house platform into and on to the ditch fills.

THE CHURCH SITE (Fig. 11)

Period Ia. The pre-church period was presumably not of long duration, as the quantity of finds was generally small and the number of features limited. Although the area was greatly disturbed by the church itself and by the cemetery to the south, two areas of occupation can be discerned. These two were divided by a north-south ditch, with smaller ditches at right angles. On the same alignment were the features of the western occupation area, post holes, sumps, a beam slot, and one possible cess pit. This pit, though its fill was not examined, was certainly not a sump, and did not contain enough domestic material to be considered a rubbish pit.

No floor levels were defined, though the eastern occupation area revealed part of a cobble spread. The areas designated were no doubt only parts of the true occupation areas. Nevertheless, the alignment of the features is important in that it coincides with that of the hollow way north of the church, not with the southern hollow way, which parallels the axis of the church.

Period Ib. The features of Period Ib had an alignment strikingly different from those of Period Ia. Their fill, too, was different, containing mortar, which was not found in the earlier features. These features, all post holes, existed immediately prior to the completion of the church, as some were cut by interior structures. The post holes may have formed a very small building, perhaps an oratory. More probable, however, is that they were supports for a scaffolding used by the builders of the church.

Period IIa. The original dimensions of the church were 39' by 14'. In its earliest phase, it was a one celled structure with north and south doors in the west half of the nave. Outside the south doorway was a pathway, along the north border of the cemetery. Around the three walls of the nave proper were flint and mortar beddings for wall benches. A depression by the west wall marked the original position of the font. However, there was no evidence of an altar, though an area of burning in the northeast corner may have marked the position of an incense burner. The floor level was mortar laid upon a bed of clunch and mortar, both of which had been badly worn away in the west nave. The graves of the first phase were all along the north wall and had no associated slabs.

Period IIb. Small structural changes occurred after the original construction. In the southeast corner, the wall bench platform was reinforced and expanded perhaps as an enclosed pew for the lord's family, though the platform for the west wall bench was also expanded. To make room for this expansion, the font was moved a few feet eastward. The graves of Period IIb covered the centre of the nave and the south. The area in front of the expanded southeast wall bench was, however, kept clear. The graves of this phase had over their heads square memorial slabs, perhaps of slate (see Worked Stone).

Period IIc. After a substantial period of time for the floor and sub-floor to have been worn away, the church was expanded and its interior features radically changed. The new dimensions of the church were 45' by 14'. A grave (F. 9) was placed in the east end of the nave, abutting the former east wall and cutting through occupation levels of Period IIb. Over this grave was constructed a step to the chancel, which was raised 6" above the new floor of the nave. No evidence of either the altar or the chancel floor was preserved, possibly the latter was of wood.

In the nave, the memorial slabs were removed and the entire surface covered by a deposit of clay over a spread of mortar from the wall construction. This clay covered everything, including the wall bench supports. No features were observed in this layer, and there was no occupation deposit upon it. This sterility is explained by several floor tiles found in the destruction debris. All were found outside the church except for a stack of five by the north doorway. The arrangement of the nave with its new tiled floor is not known. No new font soak-away was found, though the one of Period IIb was covered by the clay. No changes were noted in the doorways, but it may be in this period that a threshold outside the south door was constructed, perhaps to preserve the sill from being worn away. The pathway to the door was about a foot below the surrounding ground level.

Period III. The destruction of the church was thorough. All the floor tiles were removed from the nave, and some of the memorial carvings had been removed before extensive burning took place inside the church. The fire centered in the east nave and chancel. The east wall may have collapsed at this point as there was a thick spread of rubble eastward. It is also in this area that most of the burned stained glass and melted window

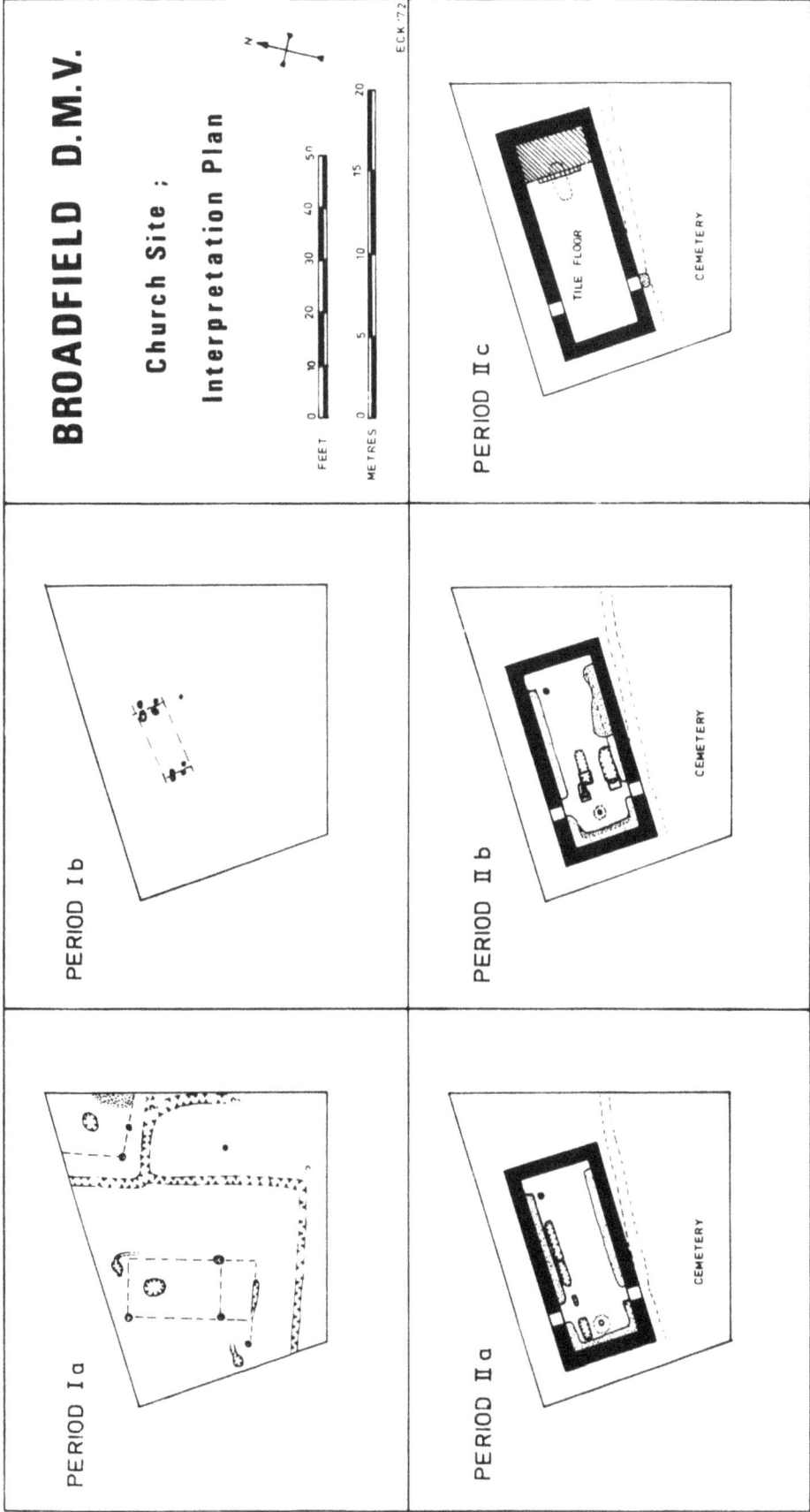

BROADFIELD D.M.V.

Church Site ;

Interpretation Plan

ECK '72

FEET   0   10   20   30   40   50

METRES 0   5   10   15   20

PERIOD I a

PERIOD I b

PERIOD II a   CEMETERY

PERIOD II b   CEMETERY

PERIOD II c   TILE FLOOR   CEMETERY

Fig. 11

lead was found; the window must have been intact when the wall fell. The roof, too, was intact before the fire as no evidence remained of a systematic removal of roof tiles. Many were found burned and shattered, having fallen off the roof as their wooden pegs caught fire.

After the fire, the walls were robbed; the local population may have used it over a period of time as a quarry for building stone. However, the sanctity of the ground may not have been completely forgotten or ignored. It may well have been at this time that the small infant burial was dug by the south wall of the church. Also, animal burials, perhaps pets of the manor household, showed that the memory of the church lingered on for many generations.

Cemetery. Aside from assigning the cemetery to Period II, no further sub-division was possible. The general limits of the cemetery were defined by several exploratory cuttings (Figs. 3, 13). There were perhaps 75 to 100 burials. All graves were orientated to the axis of the church. An order does appear; they were in parallel rows. There were at least six rows which were reused, as there were numerous examples of secondary burials. The post holes found in the cemetery may have been supports for some type of memorial structures, but it is more likely that they formed an enclosure, a boundary fence, aligned with the church. At some period in the life of the cemetery, there was an attempt to regulate its use or possibly to subdivide it into units, possibly family plots.

GENERAL INTERPRETATION

Period I. (Fig. 12) Three house plots can be distinguished. They were south of an east-west hollow way which continued to the main area of earthworks to the east. Timber houses and small toft ditches were aligned to this hollow way. One of these timber buildings was of well aligned beam slots, and was of such good construction that it may have been the manor of this period.

Period II. (Fig. 13) The insertion of a church and its surrounding enclosure destroyed all the house plots of Period I. Nevertheless, the change was not as radical as might be expected. The churchyard boundary ditches

BROADFIELD

Site Interpretation ; Period 1

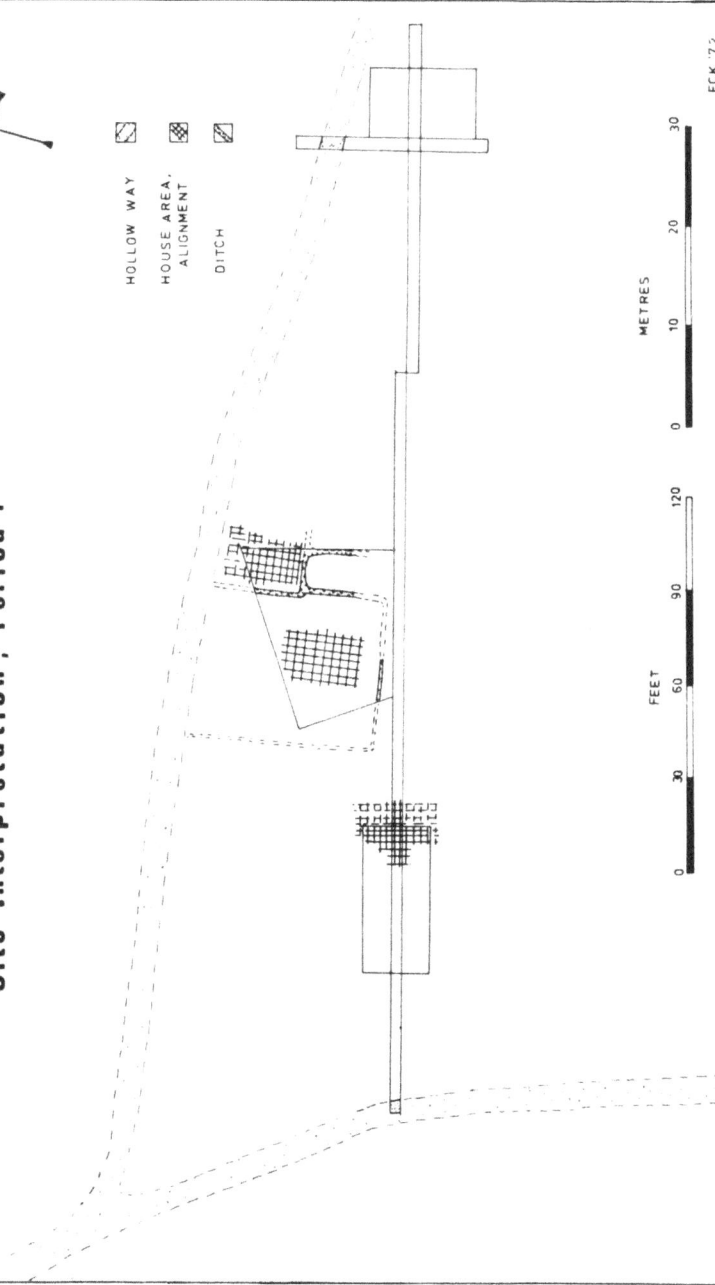

N

HOLLOW WAY

HOUSE AREA.
ALIGNMENT

DITCH

FEET

0   30   60   90   120

METRES

0   10   20   30

ECK '72

Fig. 12

were aligned to the northern hollow way, not to the orientation of the church. The domestic building, erected on the west platform at this time, followed the alignment of the ditches. However, a southern hollow way developed, running parallel to the church and superceding the hollow way of Period I, which was used as a boundary-drainage ditch. The churchyard was well ordered, divided into six rows south of the church.

Period III. The destruction of the church was followed by the filling in of one of its boundary ditches and the levelling of the adjacent peasant toft. The hollow way of Period II, after partially silting naturally, was deliberately filled in. Later features ignored the medieval village plan, though at times incorporated the earlier earthworks for drainage purposes.

Dating. Precise dating has been a serious problem. The only coins found were one of George III in the topsoil and one of Edward II in the level of church destruction. The Edwardian coin (1307-27) was badly worn and apparently lost after the church fell into disuse.

Documentary evidence is more helpful. Broadfield Church is fairly well documented in the thirteenth century, first referred to as a chapel in 1220, but as a church and rectory thereafter. The last rector to be mentioned was so in 1346. The church was 'decayed' by the sixteenth century, and its true history forgotten.

The dating of the pottery (see Appendix C) agrees with the documentary evidence. Although the village existed in 1066, and there are a few eleventh century sherds, the occupation of the site in Period Ia begins c. 1100. Period Ib was extremely brief, c. 1220. Period IIa would have begun shortly afterwards, again c. 1220. The structural changes of Period IIb would have taken place after some time, c. 1275. Period IIc has been dated mainly from the stained glass made for the extended chancel, and began c. 1340. The destruction of the church, marking the beginning of Period III, is difficult to date precisely because of the extensive destruction of the upper layers by post-medieval stone quarrying. However, it seems that the cemetery went out of use by the early fifteenth century, if not earlier; and

32

BROADFIELD

Site Interpretation ; Period 2

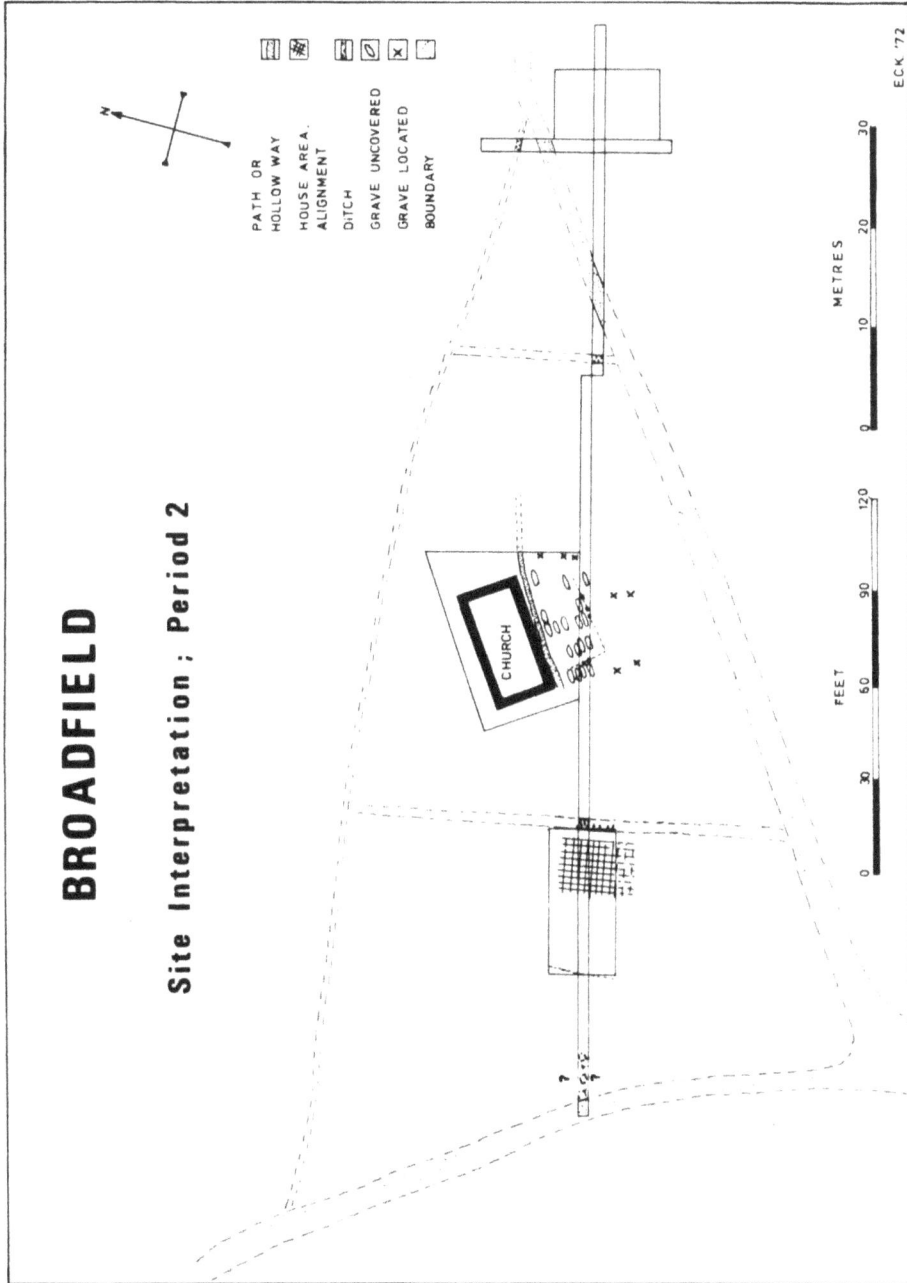

PATH OR
HOLLOW WAY
HOUSE AREA.
ALIGNMENT
DITCH
GRAVE UNCOVERED
GRAVE LOCATED
BOUNDARY

N

CHURCH

FEET

0   30   60   90   120

METRES

0   10   20   30

ECK '72

Fig. 13

while the building could have stood until the Dissolution, it is more likely that its deliberate dismantling and accidental burning took place in c. 1450.

VII. COMMENTARY

1. THE CHURCH

The nature of the church itself is worth further discussion. It cannot be determined if the building found was that chapel which existed prior to 1222, but it is certainly the church mentioned thereafter. Similarly, the rectangularly associated post holes of Period Ib would form a building too small even for a chapel or oratory. There were, moreover, no graves aligned to these features. Therefore, if the church building was not the earlier chapel, it must have been elsewhere in the village.

The church was not an exceptional structure. A parallel may be found only a mile away, at Holy Trinity Church at Throcking (see Appendix D for their comparative dimensions). Although there are minor differences, a western tower and no north door, the dimensions of the nave and presbytery at Throcking are quite similar to Broadfield's nave and chancel. At Throcking, there is a further division, a chancel, but each division is marked by a step, with no distinction in structure, again as at Broadfield.

The church has many structural parallels; certainly, its rectangular form is standard in late medieval architecture. However, among the published excavated churches, St. Mary's in Winchester shows several similarities in phases K through T with a chancel step, wall benches, and a centrally positioned font soak-away [Biddle 1968, 263-65; 1969, 306-08; 1970, 302-04]. Upon further archaeological investigation, the relationship of these details may be found to be a general development of medieval parish churches in England.

2. THE MANOR

Another point of interest is the nature of the Period I house of the west platform. This timber building had walls resting on beam sills. It was either

34

of one bay with an ancillary projection or of two bays, and the walls were at almost perfect right angles, contrasting with the more typical ill-angled houses of the rest of the site. This superior construction suggests that it was more than a simple peasant cottage. Similarly, if it were of two bays, the width would have been c. 25', well past the six metre minimum which Hurst has established for houses of "a higher social scale" [Beresford and Hurst 1971, 115]. If this, indeed, was a manor house, its relative unpretentiousness would fit the small size of the village very well.

The later manor was presumably in the present hall area. The seventeenth century records show payments for filling in the old moat and the digging of a new one [Hine 1951, 6]. There is no evidence to suggest that an earlier hall on the west platform was replaced by a moated manor on the present site. "It was not until the end of the thirteenth century that moats became common." [Beresford and Hurst 1971, 122]. If such a change did occur, a moat c. 1220 would have been extremely early. However, the churchyard ditches of Period II were much larger and deeper than the ditches of the previous period. Local climatic change may have been the cause for both occurrences. Suffice it to say, then, if the Period I building was the manor house, it was moved shortly before 1222, probably south to the present manor site where there was a medieval moat.

3. THE CHANGING PLAN

A third point of interest is the change in the village plan; from the area investigated it would seem to be considerable. There are several other instances where a church has been imposed upon a village plan: Clopton, Cambs.; Salome, Hunts.; Weald, Hunts.; Baldean, Sussex [Beresford and Hurst 1971, 178]. Medieval manors were not static; in these respects, Broadfield is no exception.

The establishment of the church would have been a single act, perhaps accomplished in a single season. The church was on a new alignment to the already existing northern hollow way. The church itself had a northern as well as a southern entrance. The northern doorway of the church was never blocked, and the northern hollow way silted up and was not deliberately filled.

However, it was the southern doorway which had the predominant use; it was the southern hollow way, aligned to the church, which replaced the northern one. The overall change in the village plan was dramatic, but it was not predetermined. Three house areas were deliberately destroyed, and a church and cemetery planted upon them; one village roadway decayed, and another replaced it. Thus, on the one hand, there was a deliberate act of replanning the village for the church (and perhaps the manor). On the other hand, the most important effect of the replanning, the change in street plan, was the result of a slow and evolutionary process.

4. THE ENVIRONMENT

As no soil samples were taken, it is not possible to establish the flora of medieval Broadfield by a pollen count. Aside from the post-medieval animal burials, no non-human bones were examined; the fauna, therefore, cannot be established either. There is some structural evidence for a climatic change, however, that of ditch construction throughout the medieval occupation.

The Period I occupation consisted of timber buildings surrounded by shallow drainage ditches. This is in keeping with what has been found elsewhere in Britain for early medieval settlements [Beresford and Hurst 1971, 117]. Broadfield is situated on boulder clay, and such ditches would relieve a minimal amount of water build-up, indicating a fairly dry climate for this area. In contrast to this, Period II marks the introduction of the deep drainage ditches. This change usually took place in the late thirteenth century [Beresford and Hurst 1971, 122]. Even the churchyard boundary ditches are of such construction, and a drainage function may be equal to that of separating consecrated land from the rest of the village. The raising of the church floor in Period IIc by a one foot thick layer of clay covered with tiles, is considerably more than necessary for a simple tile floor foundation; this also may indicate an increasingly wet climate.

The post-medieval ditch construction of Period III shows a continued effort to keep the site well drained. The east 'platform' was formed at this time by the construction of a deep ditch to the east and the recutting of the former eastern churchyard boundary ditch, while to the south ran another. The earlier northern hollow way was continually recut and used for drainage purposes. The secondary hollow way was not so treated; it was deliberately filled, also probably to increase the drainage of the area. To the west of the site, numerous ditches also show an attempt to control a high water table. Several hollows and a pond remaining in 1965 indicate a present high water table, which is in keeping with the still wet English weather.

5. THE LORDS OF BROADFIELD

The relationship of village to lord should also be considered. In the twelfth century, Broadfield had probably nucleated to the present manor, the other lands having solidified in various manors in surrounding parishes, notably Rushden. The FitzRalph family, which held the lordship, was one that grew in wealth and power throughout the Middle Ages. Though one of their original estates, Broadfield remained very much what it had always been, poor and small. The tenants' dependence upon their lords would have been great, and the FitzRalph family were of regional and local importance, as can be seen by the independence of Broadfield Church from Rushden in the early thirteenth century. Perhaps later, they became too wealthy to take a direct interest in the manor, and yet not wealthy enough to make any capital investment in it. There is no evidence for their ever having farmed out the estate.

The many transactions concerning Broadfield in the fifteenth and sixteenth centuries may only reflect the instability of the times. However, these frequent changes in landlords would have done no good to even a viable village and may well indicate that Broadfield had already failed.

6. HERTFORDSHIRE DESERTIONS

Broadfield's relationship to other Hertfordshire deserted medieval villages can only be surmised, not evaluated, as very few of the others have been excavated, and none has had more than a cursory investigation. Thus, as regards form, development, and morphology, the findings at Broadfield cannot be compared to other villages in the region. However, its position should be noted on the distribution map (Fig. 14), based on the 1968 gazet-

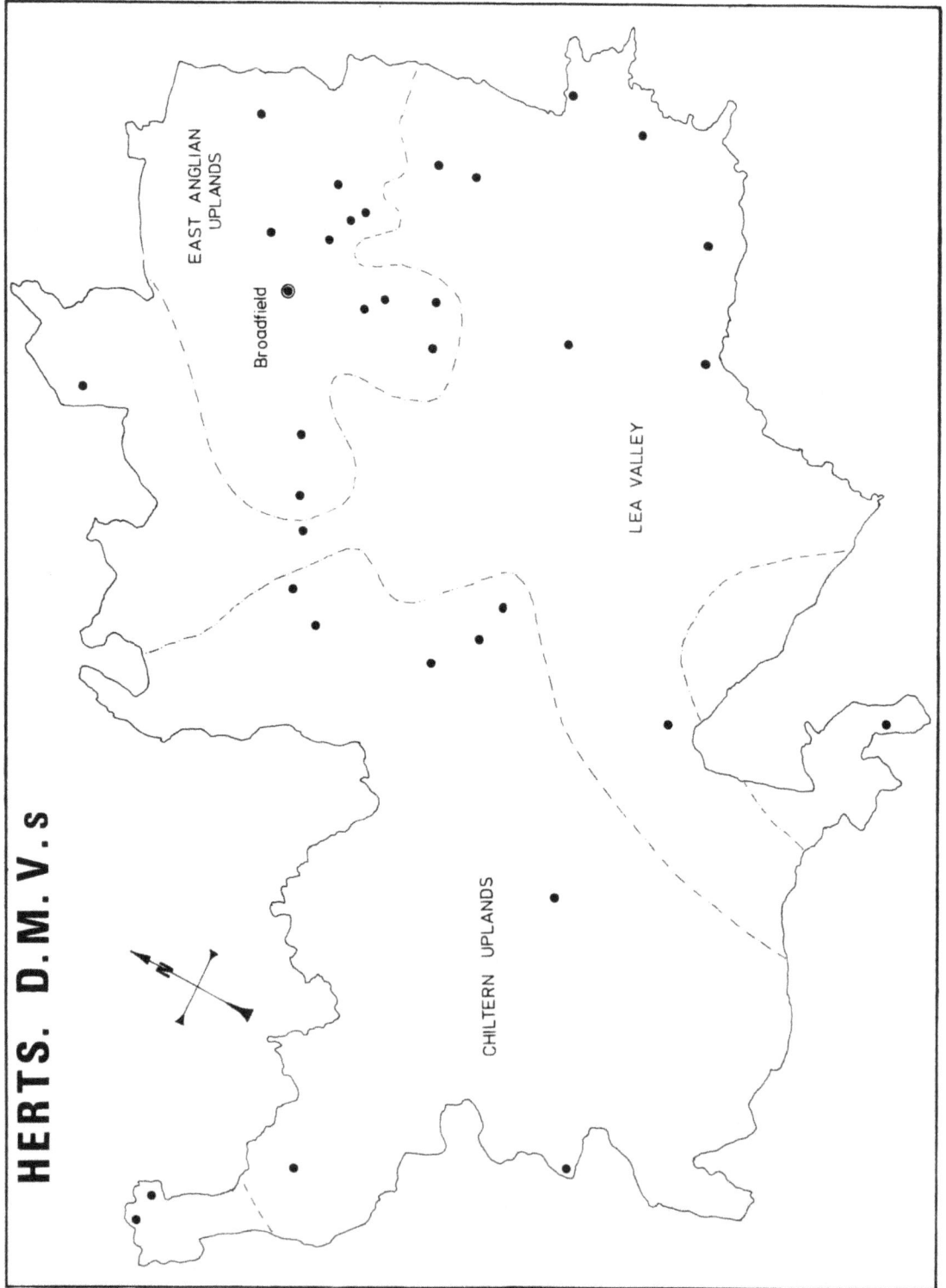

HERTS. D.M.V.s

EAST ANGLIAN
UPLANDS

Broadfield

LEA VALLEY

CHILTERN UPLANDS

Fig. 14

teer of D. M. V. 's by the Deserted Medieval Village Research Group [Beresford and Hurst 1971, 190].

Broadfield is clearly one of a group of desertions clustered in the northeast part of the county, the area of greatest desertion. This is an upland region of boulder clay, particularly susceptible to climatic changes. For this reason, one might assume that this area would be one of marginal settlement, the last to be developed, and the first to be deserted.

However, the distribution map of desertions does not take into account the settlement pattern. The northeastern part of Hertfordshire was the most heavily settled area, with a large number of villages and hamlets (Broadfield among them) in 1086. There was little room for further expansion. Thus, the Broadfield 'desertion group' is not the result of a specific geography, but rather a proportional desertion throughout Hertfordshire. There were more desertions around Broadfield simply because there were more villages. The cause should not be sought in geographic terms alone, but also for economic, social and even political reasons, a study of which can only be considered in a regional or multi-regional framework.

VIII. DESCRIPTION OF FINDS

GENERAL COMMENTS

It has not been possible to obtain quantitative analyses for the less manageable materials, i. e. worked stone and fired clay. Owing to the nature of the excavation and the lack of knowledge of environmental archaeology at the time of excavation, no soil samples, building material, nor organic specimens were collected. However, specialists have examined the stained glass, iron objects, pottery, and those skeletal remains which were taken from the site.

1.   WORKED STONE (Fig. 15)

Eight pieces of worked stone were found, all in layers associated with the church's destruction. Three are not illustrated, being too fragmentary or badly damaged to be identified. None have been examined scientifically.

Among these is a portion of a slate slab 1" thick. This was the only piece of slate found on the excavation, and would have been an import as slate is not found locally.

No. 1 (N4) Oolitic limestone. This carries a narrow central ridge from which the transverse planes are noticeably tapered (10 degrees). The reverse is continuously damaged; no original surface was left upon it. No. 1 is probably a portion of the centre of a coffin lid, with an elongated cross shaft forming the apex.

No. 2 (Church 4) Limestone. Triangular corner piece from a memorial shrine. A portion of the stone still shows strong traces of burning, interrupted by later breakage. This piece was part of a larger construction (and perhaps still in the church) when it was burned.

No. 3 (F5) Limestone. Triangular corner piece from one of the architectural features of the church. Traces of extensive burning are found on one side only of the outer face, and in one small area on the back.

No. 4 (F.10) Limestone. Well carved fragment of a base for a memorial sculpture. There are traces of burning on the originally exposed surfaces only.

No. 5 (F.10) Limestone. Portion of a human sculpture, the folds of the garment and one knee remaining. It is well carved and, no doubt, is part of the same group as No. 4. Areas of the fragment have been heavily burnt. The underside of the garment and the area above the knee are the worst burned portions. However, only original surfaces had been burned, with one small exception, indicating that this statue was at least intact from the waist down when it was burnt.

Not included with the worked stone were several fragments of lava querns found in J3, N4, N11, and N5.

2.   FIRED CLAY : FLOOR TILES
    Type A 1" to $1\frac{1}{4}$" thick, red sandy with flint inclusions up to $\frac{1}{4}$".
Opaque yellow glaze, occasionally over fired. Size: $6\frac{1}{2}$" + square; and triangular, 9" equilateral. Provenance: G2, 13, Church 1, and Church 9.

BROADFIELD WORKED STONE

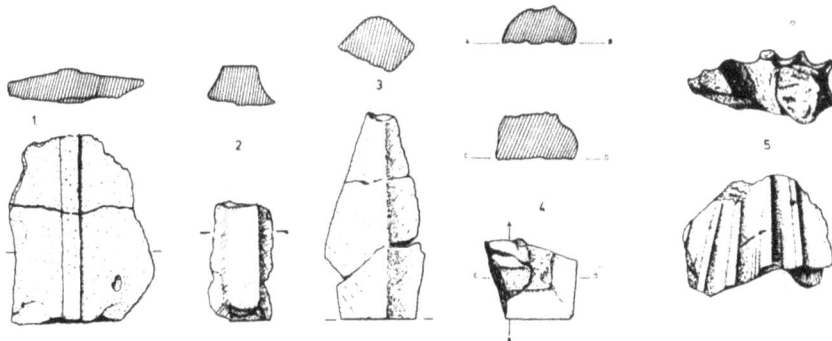

ROOF TILES

OTHER
FIRED CLAY

Illustrated Bronze

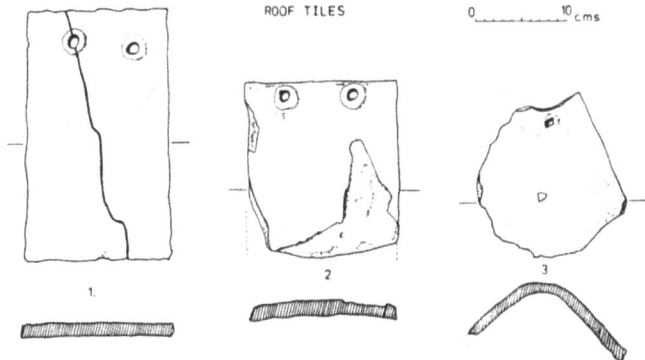

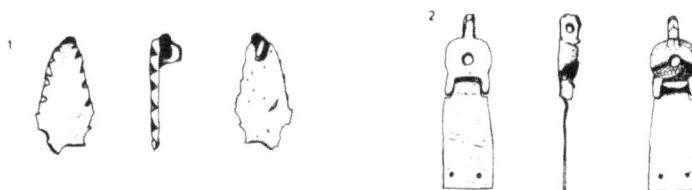

Fig. 15

Type B 1" to 1¼" thick, red sandy with flint inclusions. Black glaze. Size: 6" by 3" triangular; 6½" by ? triangular; 12¼" by 8½" triangular; and 4½" square. Provenance: F1, F3.

3.   FIRED CLAY : ROOF TILES (Fig. 15)

No. 1 (Church 4) Red sandy fabric, average thickness ½". Size: 10" by 6", slight curvature. Holes: for wooden pegs, roughly equidistant from each edge, round, made while clay not firm.

No. 2 (F4) Orange sandy fabric, average thickness 5/8". Size 7½" by 6½", strong curvature. Holes: for wooden peg, close against the short end of the tile, round, made while clay not firm.

No. 3 (Church 1) Orange sandy fabric with large flint inclusions, average thickness ½". Shape: modified ridge pole cover. Has an obliquely descending edge which joins an arc shaped edge by the hole. Hole: rectangular on top, oval on bottom, made when clay not firm, for a nail. It should fit a hipped roof, and thus would not have belonged to the church.

4.   OTHER FIRED CLAY (Fig. 15)

One piece of fired clay was found, perhaps, a fragment of a griddle. No. 1 (Church 11) Roughly black fabric with large inclusions. 1" thick with bevelled edge. Hole: made while clay not firm, by a peg inserted from the top and withdrawn, as the inside surface shows traces of clay having been pulled up over the smooth surface.

5.   POTTERY

The pottery has been typed according to fabric, with the exception of the Roman and post-medieval wares. The illustrated groups have been chosen as examples of the forms; there were no sealed groups of importance, and few pieces of intrinsic value. Phasing and stratigraphic cross referen-ces are shown in the Illustrated Pottery Table, Appendix C. The framework of this table has been found to be more valuable than detailed distribution plots. Its three components reduce the imbalance between the numerous pottery groups and the relatively few well stratified deposits, which are marked by the high rate of residual pottery to be expected on a cemetery site.

Comparative wares have been found at Hertfordshire kiln sites [Renn 1964] and at Northolt, Middlesex [Hurst 1961], but there are no close parallels. Broadfield type A may be equated with developed St. Neots ware found at Ashwell, Herts.[Hurst and Hurst 1967, 76] and Therfield, Herts. [Biddle 1964, 69]. Broadfield B_1 ware may be compared to the eleventh century sandy ware at Therfield [Biddle 1964, 70-71]. Broadfield type G is similar to the unglazed thirteenth century ware from Therfield [Biddle 1964, 79]. Finally, type H may be comparable to a white-gritted ware found at Elstree, Herts. [Biddle 1961, 69].

Mr. J. G. Hurst has kindly examined the pottery, and his comments on its dating have been underlined in the type descriptions. The long term use or re-use of local sources of clay has resulted in occasional dating problems. The lack of medieval glazed wares of any quantity is unusual, although there is a wide variety of unglazed wares. The isolation and apparent poverty of the site may be the cause of this discrepancy.

Description of Pottery

Roman There were only four small stray sherds of Roman ware, one of which was samian (Terra sigillata).

Type A (Fig. 16) Fabric: slightly soapy, buff, red-black; shell inclusions. Vessels: cooking pots, jars, bowls, platters.

Developed St. Neots ware; twelfth century

No. 1 Rim sherd of jar with infolded rim.

Nos. 2,3 Rim and base sherds respectively. Probably pieces of same small jar. Eleventh century.

Nos. 4-8 Rim sherds. Shallow, vertical sided bowls, very common, showing differences in size and lip, from straight to in-turned. No. 7 may belong to a small pot.

No. 9 Rim and shoulder sherd of large bowl.

Type B (Fig. 16) Fabric: hard, leathery ware; smooth grey to reddish brown, sometimes gritty on interior. Vessels: bowls, cooking pots, small, round, and large pots with flat lips. <u>Late thirteenth century to fourteenth century</u>.

No. 10 Rim sherd, reddish brown. Large vessel of unknown shape, wide horizontal lip. <u>Fourteenth century</u>.

Nos. 11-14 Rim sherds. Cooking pots with different quality construction and firing.

<u>Type B1</u> (Fig. 17) Fabric: similar to B, but only red or black with a deeper red especially in 'sandwich'; smooth surface. Vessels: cooking pots, bowls, platters. <u>Early medieval sandy ware; late eleventh century to early twelfth century, probably residual</u>.

Nos. 15-17 Rim sherds of small pots.

Nos. 18-19 Rim sherds of bowls.

<u>Type C</u> (Fig. 17) Fabric: pale grey, harsh sandy ware; fairly coarse with a peppered exterior, small quartzite inclusions. Vessels: two types of pots with noticeably everted rims. <u>Late twelfth century to early thirteenth century</u>.

No. 20 Rim and shoulder sherd of well made cooking pot with horizontal girth grooves. Different form from others. <u>Late thirteenth century</u>.

No. 21 Rim of sherd of cooking pot with slightly everted rim.

No. 22 Rim sherd of cooking pot with strongly everted rim.

No. 23 Rim sherd of small cooking pot with everted rim and notched lip.

<u>Type D</u> (Fig. 17) Fabric: red sandy ware with rough surface; distinctive, simple fold vertical rims. Vessels: wide mouthed bowls. <u>Twelfth century</u>.

No. 24 Rim sherd of bowl.

No. 25 Rim and body sherd of large pot with a hole directly below rim, possibly for hanging.[2]

<u>Type D1</u> (Fig. 17) Fabric: sandy, deep red, somewhat micaceous; similar to D. Vessels: bowls with simple fold flanged lip.

No. 26 (Fig. 17) Fabric: coarse grey sandy with heavily pitted surface,

---

* Holes in medieval pottery were usually for repair, but other uses were as a sieve or strainer, for hanging, or for decanting as a bunghole.

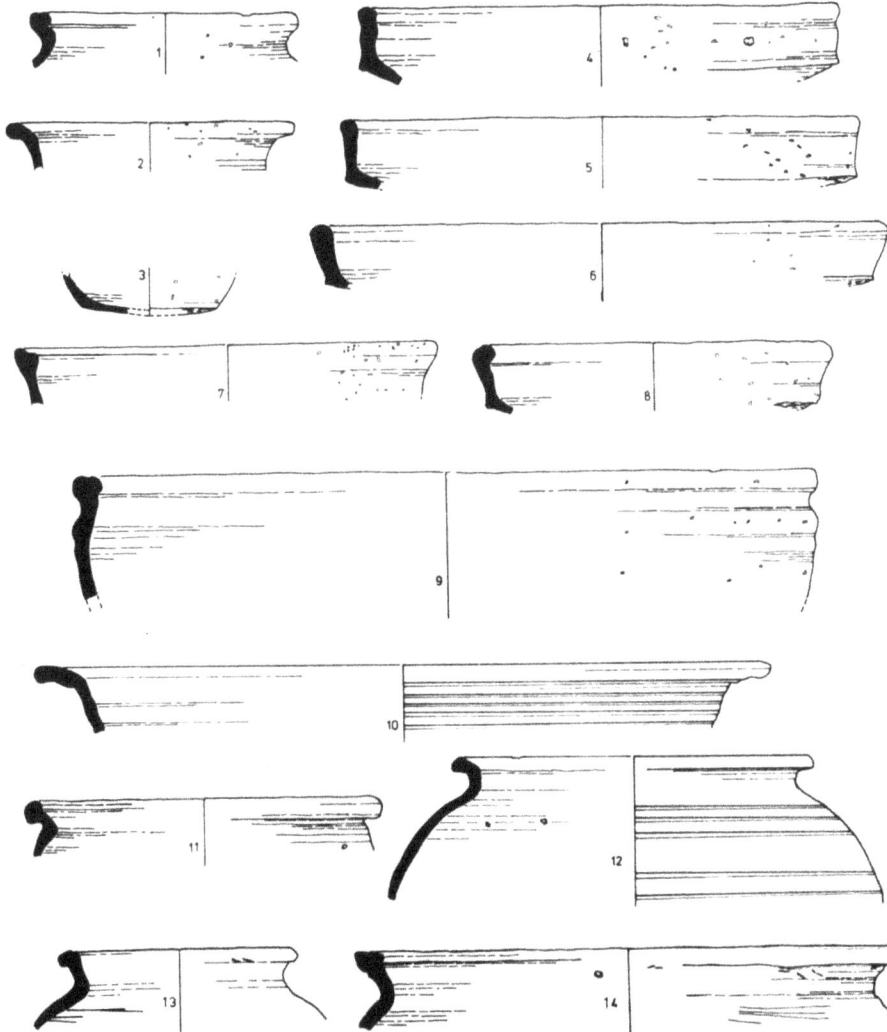

BROADFIELD

Illustrated Pottery;1

Scale $\frac{1}{4}$

Fig. 16

Type E (Fig. 17) Fabric: coarse grey sandy with heavily pitted surface, iron or ironstone inclusions. Decorated with slight horizontal ribbing and vertical thumb-pressed applied strips. Vessels: small cooking pot, others unknown. Thirteenth century.

Nos. 27, 28 Body sherds with slight horizontal ribbing and vertical thumb-pressed strip. (Black spots on the drawings represent the surface iron inclusions.)

No. 29 Rim sherd of small bowl or cooking pot. The surface is smooth, but iron inclusions appear in the broken edge.

Type F (Fig. 18) Fabric: blue-grey sandy ware, well fired, slightly micaceous with some flint inclusions. Some burnishing and incised decoration. Vessels: jugs, large pots, sub-collared jars. Late thirteenth century and early fourteenth century.

Nos. 30, 31 Rim and shoulder sherds of large cooking pots. Early fourteenth century.

No. 32-a Rim sherd of large pot.

No. 32-b Vertical view of rim No. 32-a, showing irregular incised decoration made by pointed instrument, ? bone.

No. 33 Rim sherd of collared jar with vertical lip.

No. 34 Rim sherd of collared jar, same form as No. 33 but lip has been everted.

No. 35 Lower part of jug handle, incised circular decorations made of two arcs, made by bone or quill.

No. 36 Body sherd with diagonal scoring.

Type G (Fig. 18) Fabric: dark grey, fairly coarse sandy ware, well made, micaceous. Occasional buff areas due to misfiring. Vessels: jugs, pots. Thirteenth century.

No. 37 Rim sherd of vessel with slightly everted rim and vertical lip.

No. 38 Rim sherd of cooking pot with everted rim and overhanging lip.

No. 39 Rim sherd of small cooking pot or storage vessel.

No. 40 Jug handle. From the thickness of the handle, the jug must have been quite large. Regular incised decoration made by a pointed instrument.

Type H (Fig. 18) Fabric: dark grey to dark brown, fine white gritted

46

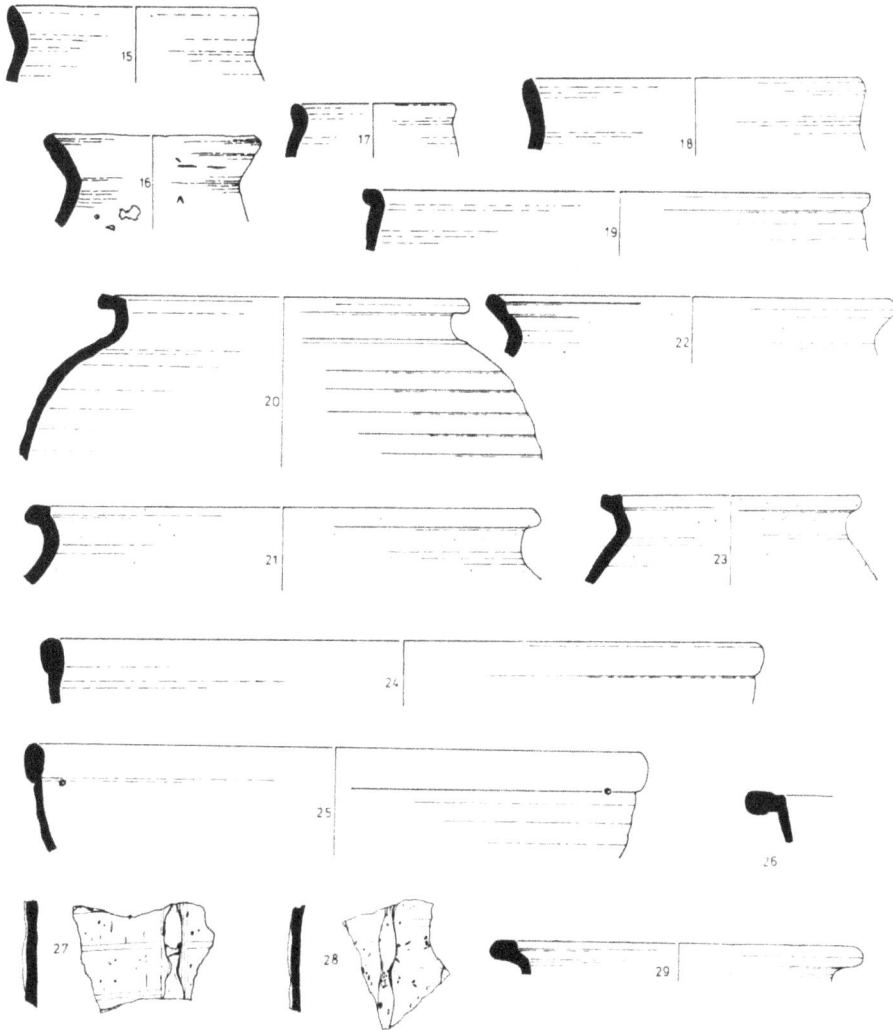

BROADFIELD   IP.2

Scale $\frac{1}{4}$

Fig. 17

47

ware; fairly coarse, especially interior. Small inclusions of quartz and shell. Vessels: small jars, small pots. Late twelfth century to early thirteenth century.

Nos. 41, 42 Rim sherds of cooking pots with lip recess.

No. 43 Rim sherds of small storage jar.

No. 45 Rim sherds of vessel with everted rim and horizontal folded lip.

Type J Fabric: micaceous, smooth, reddish sandy ware; fine, well fired, glazed interior. Vessels: large pots. Fourteenth century to fifteenth century.

Not illustrated.

Type K Fabric: rough, reddish sandy ware; poorly made, badly fired. Vessels: jug. ? Waster of thirteenth century.

Only a single sherd, part of a spout for jug, was found.

Not illustrated.

Type L (Figs. 18, 19) Fabric: combed and combed-stabbed, buff orange ware; sandy fabric liable to rub off on fingers. Poorly fired, some vessels reddish black. Vessels: collared jars, sub-collared jars, small bowls, ? jugs. Typical thirteenth century.

No. 46 Rim and body sherd of small pot, incised wavy line on body, incised decoration on rim.

No. 47 Rim and body sherd of elaborate vessel with incised wavy line on body and another on neck. Plain rim.

No. 48 Neck sherd of collared jar (? jug) with combed decoration on shoulder. Late twelfth century.

No. 49 Rim and body sherd of very small bowl with combed decoration on body and rim.

No. 50 Rim and body sherd of small bowl with comb-stabbed decoration on body below rim.

Type M (Fig. 19) Fabric: purple-grey granular, glazed ware, rough; poorly fired, often orange or black (? related to Type G). Type defined by small scattered glaze spots. Vessels: cooking pots. ? Thirteenth century.

No. 51 Base of sherd of cooking pot with sagging base and thumb-pressed

BROADFIELD   IP.3

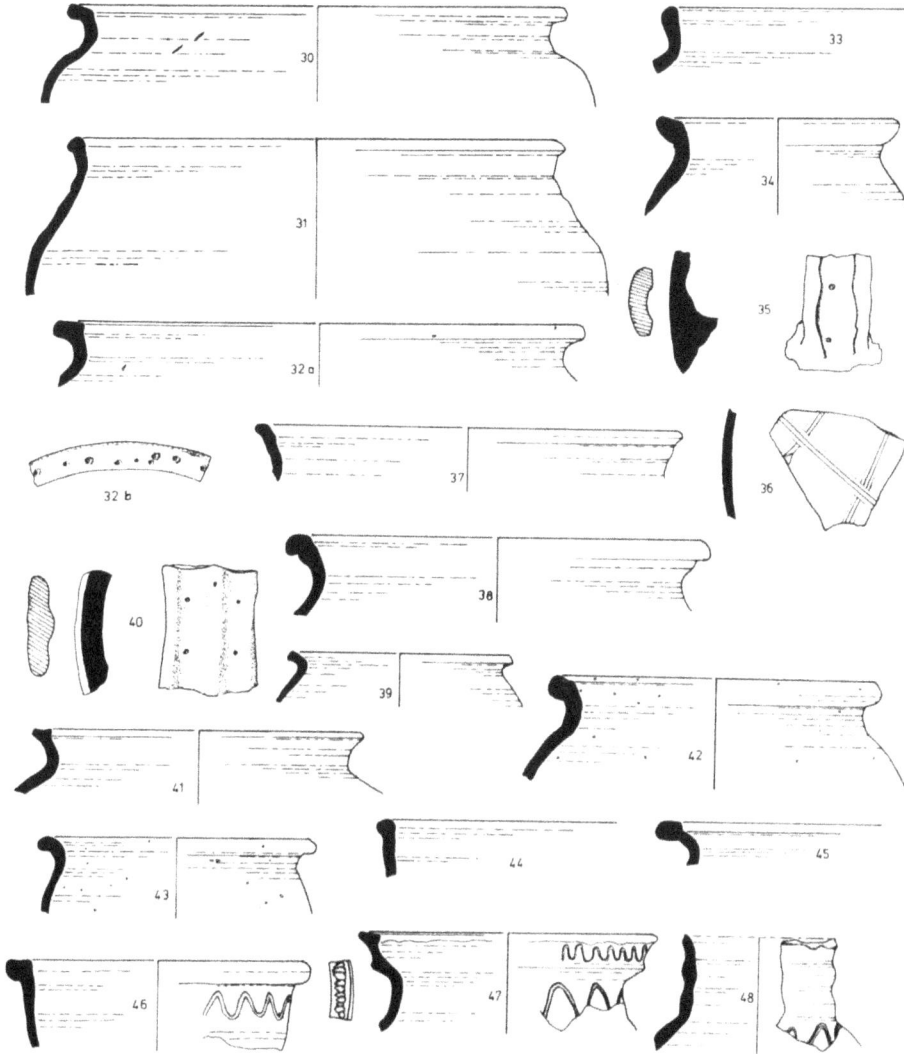

Scale ¼

Fig.   18

49

decoration on exterior.

Type N Fabric: miscellaneous glazed wares; late and post-medieval;
no rim sherds found. Vessels: ? pots, jugs.
Not illustrated.

Type O (Fig. 19) Fabric: slipped glazed ware, pale red sandy fabric;
well made and well fired. Vessels: ? pots, jugs. Late thirteenth century.
No. 52 Lower handle and shoulder piece of jug, presumably with a high
collared neck.

Type P (Fig. 19) Fabric: hard, reddish glazed ware; well made and
well fired. Vessels: jugs, large storage vessels. The discontinuity of dating is due to the use of the same fabric. Fourteenth century to sixteenth
century.
No. 53 Rim and body sherd of collared vessel with fine horizontal ribbing
on shoulder and interior ledge for lid. Green glazed ware: fifteenth century.
No. 54 Rim and body sherd of large pot.
No. 55 Body and base sherd of large storage vessel with sagging base and
bung hole. Fourteenth century.
No. 56 Rim and handle sherd of jug with thumb-pressed applied strip on
neck. Sixteenth century.
No. 57 Rim and body sherd of large pot with a horizontal lip and a strip of
applied thumb'pressed decoration on shoulder. Fourteenth century.

Type R (Fig. 19) Fabric: smooth, reddish ware without glaze; well
made and well fired, similar to Type P. Vessels: jugs, large storage
vessels.
No. 58 Rim sherd with part of handle of large jug. Fifteenth century.
No. 59 Body sherd of storage container with elaborate quatrefoil bung hole.
Fifteenth century to sixteenth century.
No. 60 Base sherd of jug or storage vessel with sagging base and elaborate
ring base. Interiorly pitted. Fifteenth century to sixteenth century.
No. 61 Base sherd of chafing dish. Fifteenth century to sixteenth century.

Type S Fabric: purple skinned (red interior), late medieval ware; well
made and well fitted. Vessels: pitchers, pots.

BROADFIELD

I P.4

inches 0 _____ 5

cms 0 _____ 10

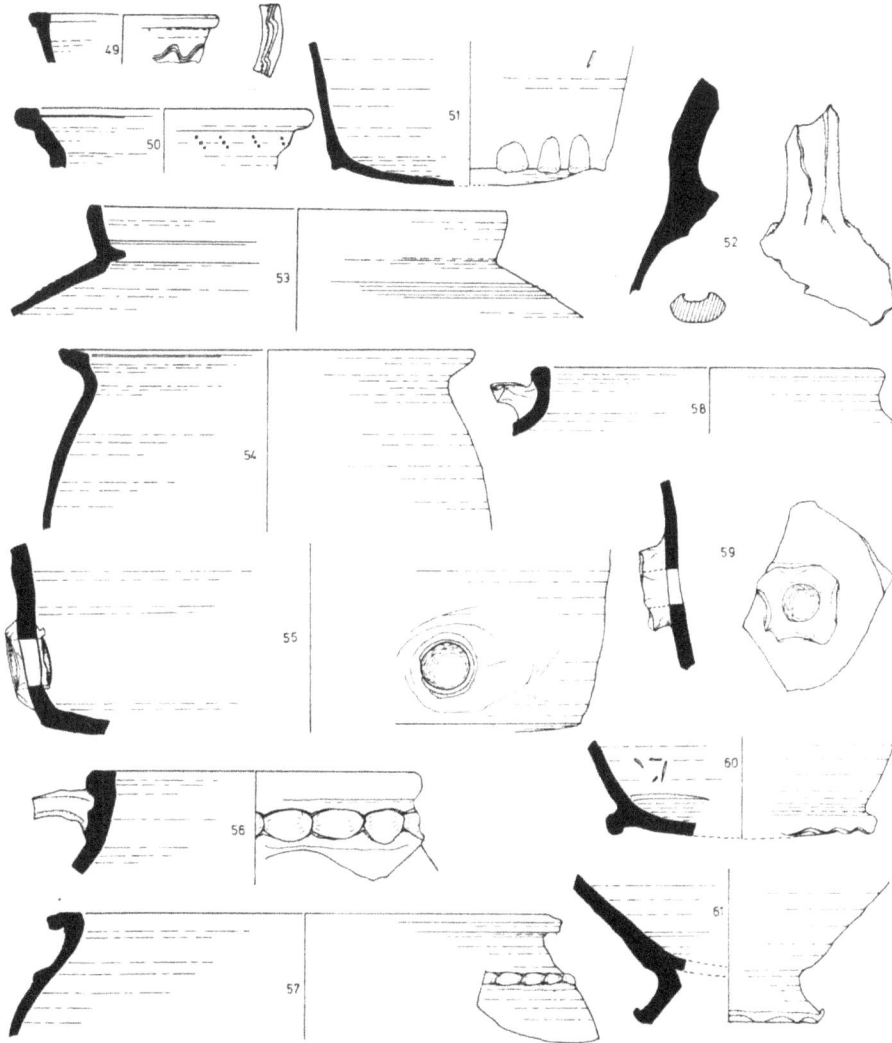

Scale ¼

Fig. 19

Not illustrated.

Type T Fabric: post-medieval brown glazed ware; well made and well fired. Vessels: pots.
Not illustrated.

Type U Fabric: post-medieval black glazed ware; well made and well fired. Vessels: jugs.
Not illustrated.

Type V Fabric: combed slip ware, post-medieval; well made and well fired. Vessels: pots.
Not illustrated.

Type X (Fig. 20) Fabric: black, smooth sandy ware, some incised decoration and burnishing; thin walled, well made, poorly fired. Vessels: large cooking pots. Late fourteenth century.
No. 62 Large thin walled deep bowl with sagging base. Exterior black, ? burnished; interior unevenly fired, some parts buff.
No. 63 Body and base sherd of cooking pot with sagging base, incised decoration on base extended to edge. Irregular light incision on body, small inclusions of quartzite and shell.
No. 64 Rim sherd of shallow vessel with horizontal lip.

Type Y (Fig. 20) Fabric: buff, coarse sandy, white gritted ware; small flint and quartzite inclusions, some decoration; ? related to Type H or Z. Thirteenth century.
No. 65 Rim sherd of large pot with thumb-pressed applied vertical strips of decoration descending from rim.

Type Z (Figs. 20, 21) Fabric: miscellaneous sandy ware, pale orange-buff, black or peppered; well made, poorly fired; some finger pressed strip decoration. Vessels: shallow bowls, small bowls, large and small cooking pots, jars. Twelfth century to fourteenth century.
No. 67 Rim and body sherd of shallow bowl (see Type A) with sagging base and more pronounced ribbing. Everted lip on inverted rim.
No. 68 Rim and body sherd of small shallow bowl (see Type A) with sagging

BROADFIELD

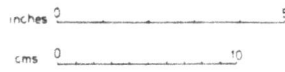

I P.5

inches 0 _____ 5

cms 0 _____ 10

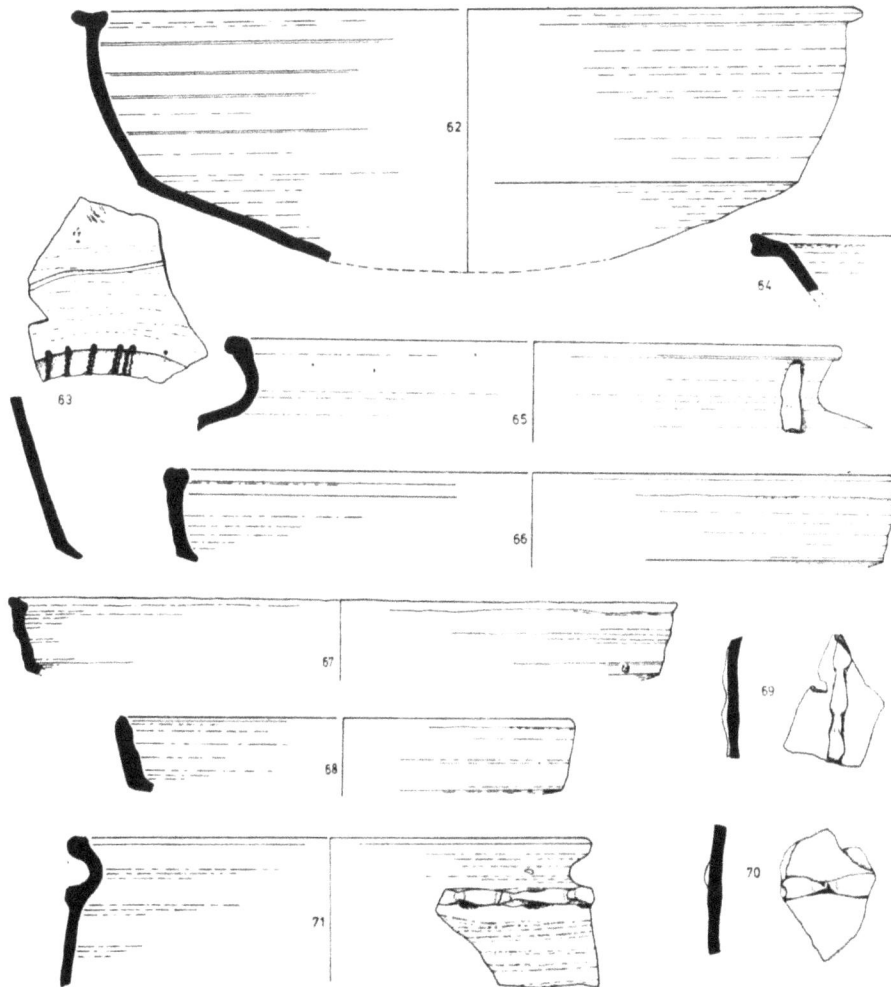

Scale $\frac{1}{4}$

Fig. 20

base and no ribbing. Vertical rim and plain lip.

Nos. 69, 70 Body sherds with thumb-pressed applied strip decoration, horizontal and vertical, similar to Type E.

No. 71 Rim and body sherd of large pot with horizontal thumb-pressed applied strip decoration on shoulder.

No. 72 Rim sherd of large vessel with thumb-pressed decoration on out turned rim. Only one example found. Twelfth century.

Nos. 73, 74 Rim and body sherds of small bowls.

Nos. 75-78 Rim sherds of large, wide mouthed pots with high necks, showing a change in rims from vertical to strongly everted.

Nos. 79-83 Rim and body sherds of smaller cooking pots. Series shows different divisions between rim and shoulder, and the neck as a distinct feature.

No. 84 Rim and body sherd of cooking pot with turned down lip and subsequent overhang.

No. 85 Rim and body sherd of cooking pot with strong horizontal lip and a distinctive incised line between shoulder and neck. Only example of this form.

6.   GLASS (Fig. 22)

Large quantities of fragmented and vitrified window glass were found in the destruction layer at the east end of the church. Some stained glass was found, and the identifiable pieces are illustrated.

Dr. P. A. Newton, who examined the glass, considers that the evidence is slight and by no means conclusive. The fragments of canopy and foliage suggest a dating c. 1300 - 1350, probably more likely in the second quarter of the century.

No. 1 (Church 7) Foliage design. One curved edge remains.

No. 2 (Church 3 - F. 10) Uncertain design. One edge remains.

No. 3 (Church 3 - F. 10) Possible fragment of canopy. Three edges remain of trapezoidal pane.

No. 4 (Church 3 - F. 10) Piece of background foliage design: part of two trefoil leaves. Three edges remain of rectangular pane. Fourteenth century.

BROADFIELD

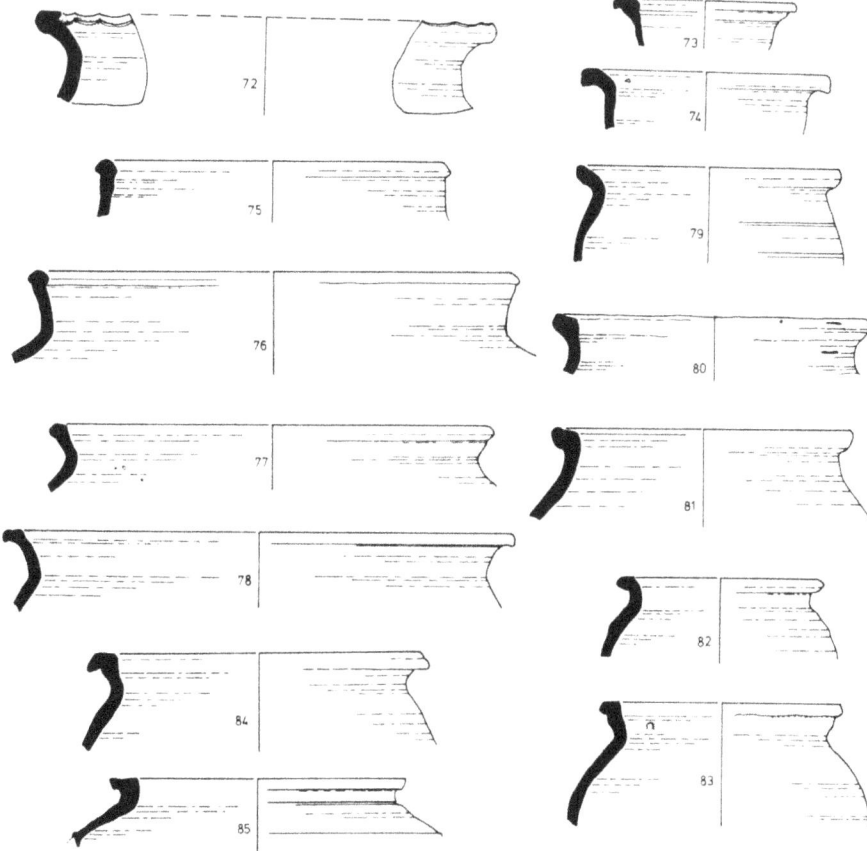

Scale ¼

Fig. 21

No. 5 (Church 7) Uncertain design. Three edges remain of narrow rectangular pane.

No. 6 (Church 3- F.10) Uncertain design, perhaps foliage. No edges
remain.

No. 7 (Church 3 - F.10) Foliage design. One curved edge remains.

No. 8 (Church 3) Small portion of tracery design: a quatre-foil, surmounted
by a crocketed gable. Two curved edges remain. Fourteenth century.

No. 9 (Church 7) Elaborate fleur-de-lis, size indicates that it was probably
from a border design of a main light. Three edges remain of rectangular
pane. Fourteenth century.

No. 10 (Church 3 - F.10) Framed Gothic script; the letters may be 'SON'.
The tight vertical form of the letters suggest a date not earlier than mid-
fourteenth century. Two edges remain of rectangular pane.

No. 11 (Church 7) Similar to No. 8. Two edges remain of quadrant-shaped
pane.

7.   IRON OBJECTS (Fig. 22) by Ian H. Goodall

All objects have been X-rayed. The cutler's marks of knives 1 and 4
are drawn at full size by each knife in Fig. 22.

No. 1 I.O.4 (G5) Knife, pointed tang and blade broken. Cutler's mark,
inlaid with non-ferrous metal, on the blade.

No. 2 I.O.6 (I3) Knife blade with angled back, incomplete.

No. 3 I.O.2 (O1) Knife, pointed tang and blade broken.

No. 4 I.O.3 (G5) Knife, strip tang and blade incomplete. The tang retains
two iron rivets and part of one of the bone scales of the handle, decorated
with ring and dot ornament. Two rectangular bands, slightly out of register,
revealed by the X-ray represent non-ferrous solder which held shoulder
plates in position in front of the handle. Their position is stippled on the
drawing. Cutler's mark, without inlay, on the blade.

No. 5 I.O.7 (J3) Stud, raised head and wedge-shaped shank.

No. 6 I.O.11 (N9) Object of rectangular section with clenched tang, prob-
ably a rake or harrow prong. A similar object is known from Cropston,
Leics., a site which produced material principally of post-medieval date
[Clarke 1952, 42-43].

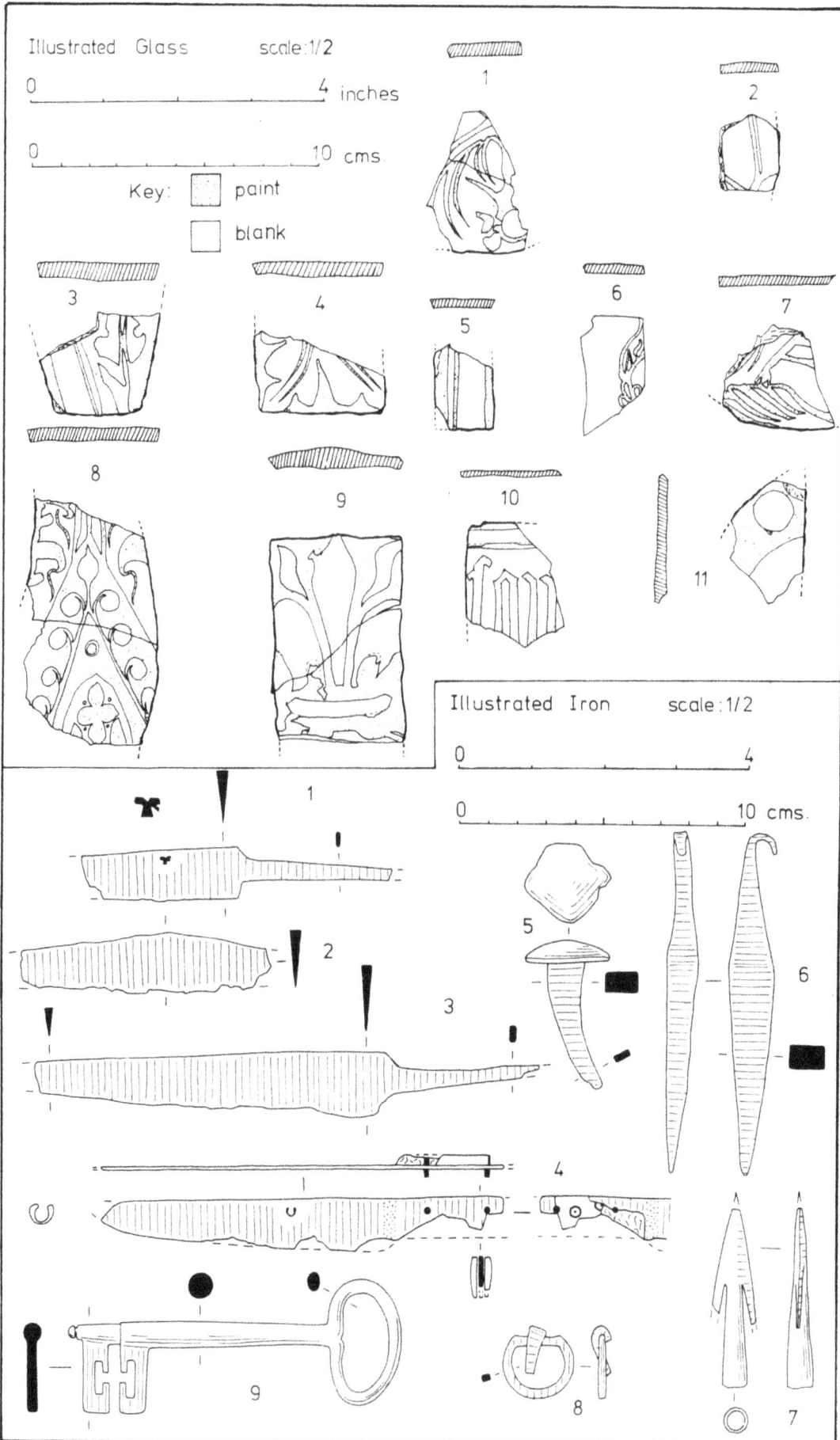

Illustrated Glass   scale:1/2

0 _____ 4 inches

0 _____ 10 cms.

Key: paint

         blank

1

2

3

4

5

6

7

8

9

10

11

Illustrated Iron   scale:1/2

0 _____ 4

0 _____ 10 cms.

1

2

3

4

5

6

7

8

9

Fig. 22

57

No. 7 I.O.12 (N10) Socketed and barbed arrowhead.

No. 8 I.O.5 (G3) D-shaped buckle, pin broken with non-ferrous plating.

No. 9 I.O.9 (B10) Key with a slightly kidney-shaped bow, swollen stem, stopped above the bit, and a knobbed end. The form of the bow is found on medieval keys, but the slightly baluster-shaped stem and terminal knob are more characteristically post-medieval. Probably sixteenth or seventeenth century.

8. BRONZE OBJECTS (Fig. 15)

No. 1 (Church 8) Belt chape or brooch with serrated decoration. Remains of an iron pin extend through underside projection.

No. 2 (Unstratified) Belt chape with stamped decoration and loop for pendant. Fifteenth or sixteenth century [Med. Cat. 1940 ed., 269, No. A.2553].

No. 3 (F.62) $\frac{1}{4}$" thick fragment of bronze, curved smooth surfaces with some bronze nodules attached to the outer surfaces. ? Church fitting. Not illustrated.

9. LEAD

Numerous lead scraps were found among the destruction debris of the church. Most could be identified as window cames, and many had been twisted and melted by fire.

10. COINS

No. 1 (B2) George III copper half penny, 1770-1775 [Brook 1932, 230, Pl. LV, No. 1]. Reverse has been erased and the initials W.M.O.D. inscribed. Possibly used as a keepsake. Not illustrated.

No. 2 (Church 3) Edward II silver half penny, London mint, 1307-1327 [Brook 1932, 123-24; C.B.M. 1960, 46, Pl. VIII, No. 255]. Stamped offset to lower left, badly worn. Most of surface smooth, very thin with cracks. Not illustrated.

11. THE HUMAN BONES   by C. R. Oyler, M.D.

Infant Burial, F.14

The bones present were chiefly fragmented, though those of the long bones were complete, except for the epiphyses. Reconstruction was virtually impossible. A single skeleton only was represented, that of a baby at full-term. The age can be given as anything between 0-3 months from birth. One cannot assess the sex, nor can one say whether or not this baby ever lived. It may have been a still birth.

Grave 1, Trench H

A. The Skull

Condition: The skull bones were very fragmented but it was found possible to reconstruct most of the cranium, though the bones of the face and maxilla were entirely missing. Such fracturing of skull bones follows from collapse at the time of excavation and also from pressure under the soil, particularly in the case of shallow burials in farmland where heavy machinery may from time to time pass over the burial. A typical partial fracture due to soil pressure is seen in the left parietal bone and the resultant distortion, though slight, has meant that there is a failure to align the two parietal bones at the sagittal suture.

Description: It is a small, thin walled, skull and the sutures are not fused. In the past it has been stated that the skull sutures fuse with advancing age, but this is no longer accepted as a tenable guide to assessing the age of an individual. In this particular case, senility has probably played a part in the separation of the individual bones at their suture lines.

Delineation: There is no doubt that this is the skull of a woman, from the following evidence:

> Faintly marked muscle insertions.
> Small supraorbital ridges.
> Small occipital crest and faint nuchal lines.
> Posterior root of the zygomatic process does not extend behind the margin of the external auditory meatus.
> Very small mastoid processes.
> Very faint parietal lines.

Pathology: There is no evidence of damage or disease in life and the only anomaly is a small nodule over the right frontal bone. This sort of reaction may occur around a foreign body (eg. a gun-shot pellet in a more modern age) but there is no sign of anything included in what appears to be solid bone on cutting through part of it. It must be regarded as an anomaly of unknown cause and of little significance.

B. The Mandible

The mandible is almost complete though the condyles are missing. It is a fairly 'senile' bone as is shown by the wide angle between the body and the rami and this is confirmed by the considerable wear (attrition) of the teeth.

The molar and pre-molar teeth are lost and it is apparent that they were lost some years before death, shown by the healed state of the alveolar bone. In addition there has obviously been much chewing on the toothless gums. The wide, splayed out, configuration of the jaw in the region of the missing teeth bears witness to this and the jaw has also become unusually muscular for someone who must otherwise have been a slight, aged female.

It is very difficult to assess the age of this individual from features which are normally taken as the most important in making this determination. The wear on the remaining teeth, for example, is probably much greater than it would otherwise be owing to the absence of the molars to take some of the share of the work. The chewing on the gums leaves an altered bony shape and thus makes the usual comparisons untenable. The absence of the maxilla prevents observation of the dental apposition. However, assuming that 'senile' is the only safe age to give this individual, one may guess the age to be in the region of 65 years or more.

C. The Lower Limbs

The following were identifiable:

> The shafts of a left and a right femur.
> The articular heads of the two femora.
> The greater part of a left and a right tibia.
> Fragments of metatarsals and fibula.

These bones are very slender and the muscle insertions are poorly marked; they confirm the female skeletal structure. No pathological features were found in any of these bones and no evidence of osteomalacia or calcium loss.

D. The Pelvis

The remains of the pelvis were much fragmented and it was not possible to attempt any reconstruction. However, the salient points were definable and there is no doubt that this represents a typically female pelvis and is that of a small woman.

E. The Upper Limbs

The following were identified:

> The shafts of the left and right humeri.
> Fragments of the shafts of the left and right ulnae and of the
> left and right radii.
> Fragments of various carpal and metacarpal bones.

The form of these bones conforms with those already described. The right

sided bones - especially the radius - are significantly larger than the left,

indicating a strongly right handed individual.

F. Miscellaneous

Also present in the grave fill were the following:

> A 'peg' tooth not fitting the Grave 1 mandible.
> Fragments of vertebrae. Osteoarthritis was noted on the mar-
> gins of the articular surfaces of two vertebrae.
> Fragments of ribs.
> Various minute skull fragments.
> Small fragments of a scapula.
> A left clavicle. This is essentially female in character except
> for the greatly increased acromial curve. The dimensions
> suggest that this bone is from the same body as the skull.

G. Osteometric Data

The measurements are very limited owing to the fragmentation of the

remains. The tibial and femoral lengths are projections of the existing frag-

ments.

Skull

Max. cranial breadth	13.4 cm.
Max. cranial length	18.0 cm.
Cephalic Index (breadth/length x 100)	74.4 cm.
Basio-bregmatic height	12.8 cm.

Mandible

Bigonial breadth	10.2 cm.
Foramen Mentale breadth	4.4 cm.

Limbs

Femur (approximate)	41.5 cm.
Tibia (approximate)	33.0 cm.
Estimated stature of the individual:	
based on femur	156.61 cm.

Estimated stature of the individual (cont.):
    based on tibia   157.23 cm.
    based on femur plus tibia   156.76 cm.

Osteometric conclusions: a dolichocephalic (long headed) individual with a height in life of about 5' 1½".

H. Summary

The bones are without doubt those of a woman. It is worth mentioning that they are outstandingly female in character and not, as so often is the case, of doubtful sex.

The individual was elderly at the time of her death. Not so clear however is the estimation of age within a year or so. The condition of the teeth, the absence of the molars and pre-molars some time before death and the obvious chewing on the healed gums present difficult problems. The overall appearance of the mandible suggests 'senile' as the correct age, but senile is not in fact an age; it is a state. One has therefore to guess the age on very arbitary evidence and - bearing this in mind - an age of 65 might be realistic. It is however quite possible that this figure is too low.

Other than some very mild osteoarthritis - much less than one would expect in a body of the assumed age - there was nothing pathological to be found in these bones. The remarkable flattening of the alveolar surfaces of the mandible and the unusually curved acromial end of the scapula could be explained by early calcium loss, but there was no other evidence of this.

Thus, the Grave 1 skeleton was that of a small woman, about 65 years old and c. 5' 1½" tall. The remains showed no signs of injury or disease.

APPENDICES

Abbreviations

(According to The Oxford Dictionary of English Place-Names)

Ann Mon	Annales Monastici
Ch	Calendar of Charter Rolls
DB	Domesday Book London, 1783 - 1816
FA	Calendar of Feudal Aids
Fine	Calendar of the Fine Rolls
Ipm	Calendar of Inquisitiones post mortem
LRS	Publications of the Lincoln Record Society
Misc	Calendar of Inquisitions Miscellaneous
Pat	Calendar of Patent Rolls
VCH	Victoria County History, Hertfordshire
VE	Valor Ecclesiasticus
Warden	The Cartulary of the Cistercian Abbey of Old Warden, Bedfordshire, G. Herbert Fowler, ed., Manchester University Press, 1931

APPENDIX A

Chronological References to Broadfield Estates

Broadfield Manor

Year	Landowner	Source	Subject
1086	Theobald I	DB, I, 141b.	Holds 1 hide and 1/4 virgate.
1130	Fulk I	VCH, III, 210.	
1159	Theobald II and William I	Warden, No. 79.	Endowment to Warden Abbey.
c.1200	Fulk II	Warden, No. 80.	Confirmation of grant.
1203		Cur, V, 139.	Manor described as 1/2 knight's fee.
1222	Ralph I	Hugh de Welles, LRS, No. 4,III,34.	Presentation to church.
c.1260	Ralph II and Maud	Pat, 50 Henry III, 526.	Manor granted to Maud for life.
1275	Ralph	Misc. I, 218.	Manor worth 6 marks.
1303	William II	FA, II, 433.	1/2 knight's fee of Thomas de Chalers
1336		Misc, II, 372.	Hailstorm destroyed all corn.
1345	William III	Ipm, VIII, 417.	Land transaction.
1357	Margaret and Sybil	Pat, 31 Edward III, 647.	Thief cut down 32 oaks.
1359	William IV	Misc, III, 128.	Son of William III.
1386	William ? V	VCH, III, 210.	
1402	William ? V	Fine, 4 Henry IV, 188.	A tax collector for Hertfordshire.
1428	William ? VI	VCH, III, 210.	John Clerk inherits upon William's death.

Shingay Manor

Year	Landowner	Source	Subject
1086	Earl Roger Montgomery	DB, I, 137b.	Holds 1/2 hide.
1140	Sybil	VCH, III, 268.	Gives to Knights Hospitallers.

Shingay Manor (Cont.)

Year	Landowner	Source	Subject
1198	Knights Hospitallers	VCH, III, 268.	Fined for receiving thief.

Broadfield Grange

Year	Landowner	Source	Subject
1159	Warden Abbey	Warden, No. 344e; Pat, 24 Henry VII, 616.	Given 30 acres from Broadfield.
1199	Warden Abbey	Warden, No. 80; Ch, 14 Edward I, 335.	Richard I confirms grant.
1199-1203	Warden Abbey	Warden, No. 80.	Fulk confirms grant.
1200-1210	Warden Abbey	Warden, No. 81.	18 acres from Therfield.
1200-1210	Warden Abbey	Warden, No. 84.	6 acres from Rushden.
1200-1220	Warden Abbey	Warden, No. 86.	6 acres from Sandon.
1200-1220	Warden Abbey	Warden, No. 89.	2 acres from Sandon.
c.1220	Warden Abbey	Warden, No. 103.	15 acres from Rushden.
1252	Warden Abbey	Warden, No. 344f.	Henry III grants free warren.
1291	Warden Abbey	VCH, III, 267.	Grange accessed at Ll 19s. 81/4d.

Cumberlow Green

Year	Landowner	Source	Subject
1086	Robert, Bishop of Chester	DB, I, 135b.	Holds 1 virgate
1277	Roger de Somery	Pat, 5 Edward I, 193.	Minority custody given to king's aunt.
1287	John de Wengham	Pat, 25 Edward I, 316.	Deer stolen from park.

Cumberlow Green (Cont.)

Year	Landowner	Source	Subject
1303	John de Wengham	FA, II, 433.	Described as 1/4 knight's fee.
1346	Walter de Mauney	Ipm, VIII, 489.	100 acres, 1/4 kinght's fee.
1361	John de Ellerton	Ch, 35 Edward III, 169.	Edward III grants free warren.
1376	Sir Walter Lee	VCH, III, 268.	Quit-claimed land.
1428	John Clerk	FA, II, 447.	1/2 knight's fee, which Walter Mauney held once.

APPENDIX B

Chronological References to Broadfield and Rushden Churches

Broadfield Church

Year	Curate	Source	Subject
1220	?	Hugh de Welles, LRS, No. 4, III, 34.	Chapel independent of Rushden.
1222	Master Alexander Falcon	Hugh de Welles, LRS, No. 4, III, 40.	Presented to "ecclesia" by Ralph I.
1239	Stephan, Chaplain	Robert Grosseteste, LRS, No. 10, 262.	Presented to rectory by Ralph I.
1244	Robert, Chaplain	Robert Grosseteste, LRS, No. 10, 288.	Presented to rectory by Ralph I.
1247	Baldwin, Subdeacon	Robert Grosseteste, LRS, No. 10, 290.	Presented to rectory by Ralph I.
1277	Simon de Stocton, Chaplain	Richard Gravesend, LRS, No. 31, 187.	Presented to rectory by Ralph II.
1346	John Dawe, Rector	Misc, II, 500.	One of group of local clergy.
1518		LRS, No. 33.	Visitation omitted.
1530		LRS, No. 35.	Visitation omitted.
1535		VE, IV, 278.	Rectory worth only 10s.
1553		VE, IV.	Not in inventory.
1580		VCH, III, 211.	Advowson still included in sale of manor.

Rushden Church

Year	Curate	Source	Subject
c.1220	Thomas, Clerk	Warden, No. 86.	Witness to grant by Robert Basset.
1220	Andrew, Clerk	Hugh de Welles, LRS, No. 4, III, 34.	Presented to "ecclesia" by William Basset
1241	Robert de Rhuddlan, Subdeacon	Robert Grosseteste, LRS, No. 10, 277.	Presented to rectory by Dunstable Priory.
1241	Robert of Rhuddlan, Parson	Ann Mon (Dunstable), III, 158.	King supports priory's rights of presentation.

Rushden Church (Cont.)

Year	Curate	Source	Subject
1272	Robert of Scarborough	Ann Mon (Dunstable), III, 254.	Presented by priory against Basset claimant.
1288	John, nephew of Robert	Ann Mon (Dunstable), III, 342.	Presented by priory without difficulty.
1310	?	VCH, III, 270.	Given to chapter of Lincoln Cathedral.
1336	John Sampson, Vicar	R.A., LRS, No. 29, 391.	Rectory becomes vicarage.

APPENDIX C

Illustrated Pottery Table

Type	Number	Period I	Provenance Period II	Period III
A	1	15-F.51		
	2	F.42		
	3	F.42		
	4	15		
	5	15		
	6	05		
	7	05		
	8			L3
	9	F.51		3
B	10			N5
	11			4
	12		8	
	13	15		
	14	05		
B$_1$	15		8	
	16			99 (East Platform Ditch)
	17		F.27	
	18		F.4a	
	19		8	
C	20		8	
	21	F.55		
	22	15		
	23	15		
D	24			G3
	25			F.28
D$_1$	26			3
E	27		8	
	28		8	
	29		G5	
F	30			3
	31		F.9	
	32		8	
	33		8	
	34	F.42		
	35		N4	
	36			N2
G	37		8	
	38		8	
	39		8	
	40		N4	
H	41	F.35		
	42		05*	

* 05 represents the fill of a period I beam slot and a Period II post hole.

Type	Number	Provenance		
		Period I	Period II	Period III
	43	F. 42		
	44	15		
	45	F. 52		
L	46	05		
	47	F. 47	F. 4a	
	48			2
	49		8	
	50	F. 47		3
M	51		8	
O	52			N5
P	53			3
	54		8	
	55			F. 10-3
	56			F. 6-4-1
	57		8	
R	58			N2
	59			3
	60			3
	61			4
X	62		9	
	63		8	
	64		8	
Y	65		N11	
Z	66	15		
	67	F. 47		
	58	15		
	69		8	
	70		8	
	71		8	
	72		F. 13	
	73			N2
	74		Grave 1	
	75	F. 47		
	76	F. 47		
	77	F. 42		
	78		8	
	79		8	
	80		N11	
	81		N11	
	82		F. 29	
	83	F. 42		
	84	15		
	85		8	

APPENDIX D

A Note on Throcking Church

Holy Trinity Church at Throcking, only about a mile away from Broadfield, is comparable in its basic dimensions with Broadfield Church. There is no distinction in structure between chancel and nave. The walls are now plastered over but are probably of flint. The tower, supposedly thirteenth century, was constructed of flint with worked sandstone quoins. There was no north door, as opposed to Broadfield. However, the south door has clunch jambs similar to the widespread use of clunch in Broadfield Church. Holy Trinity Church has seating for approximately 50 persons.

Comparative Dimensions

Nave width   19'2"   Nave width   22'6"
Nave length   32'   Nave length 31'3"
Chancel width   19'2"   Choir width 22'6"
Chancel length 10'   Choir length 12'4"

BIBLIOGRAPHY

1. Beresford, 1969   M. Beresford, The Lost Villages of England
                             (London 1954, 6th imp. 1969).

2. Beresford and Hurst,   M. Beresford and J. C. Hurst, Deserted
        1971   Medieval Villages (London 1971)

3. Biddle, 1961   M. Biddle, "Medieval Pottery from Elstree",
                             Trans. St. Albans Archit. and Archaeol. Soc.
                             (1961), 65 - 69.

4. Biddle, 1964   M. Biddle, "Excavation of a Motte and Bailey
                             Castle at Therfield, Herts.", J. Brit. Archaeol.
                             Ass. XXVII (1964), 53 - 91.

5. Biddle, 1968   M. Biddle, "Excavations in Winchester",
                             Antiq. J. XLVIII (1968), 253 - 265.

6. Biddle, 1969   M. Biddle, "Excavations in Winchester",
                             Antiq. J. XLIX (1969), 295 - 329.

7. Biddle, 1970   M. Biddle, "Excavations in Winchester",
                             Antiq. J. XL (1970), 277 - 326.

8. Brooke, 1932   G. C. Brooke, English Coins (London 1932).

9. Brigg, 1895   W. Brigg, ed., The Herts. Geneologist and
                             Antiquary I (1895)

10. C. B. M., 1960   Coins of the British Museum, published by the
                             Trustees (1960).

11. Clarke, 1952   D. T-D. Clarke, "Archaeology in Leicester-
                             shire 1939-51", Trans. Leics. Archaeol. Soc.
                             XXVIII (1952), 42 - 43; Jewry Wall Museum,
                             Leicester, Acc. No. 21.1944.

12. Hine, 1951   R. L. Hine, Relics of an Uncommon Attorney
                             (London 1951).

13. Hurst, 1961   J. C. Hurst, "The Kitchen Area of Northolt
                             Manor, Middlesex", Medieval Archaeol. V
                             (1961), 211 - 300.

14. Hurst and Hurst, 1967   D. G. and J. C. Hurst, "Ashwell Moat", J. Brit.
                             Archaeol. Ass. Ser. 3, XXX (1967).

15. Med. Cat., 1940   "Medieval Catalogue", London Museum Cata-
                             logue No. 7 (1940, repr. 1967).

BIBLIOGRAPHY (Cont.)

16. Munby,   L. M. Munby, "Deserted Medieval Villages in Hertfordshire", Herts. Past and Present II (1961), 11 - 16.

17. Norden, 1903   John Norden, A Description of Hertfordshire (London 1903 repr.).

18. Rahtz, 1958   P. A. Rahtz, "Holworth, Medieval Village Excavation, 1958", Proc. Dorset Nat. Hist. and Archaeol. Soc. LXXXI (1959), 127 - 147.

19. Rahtz, 1969   P. A. Rahtz, "Upton, Gloucester, 1964-1968, Second Report", Trans. Bristol and Gloucestershire Archaeol. Soc. LXXXVIII (1969), 74 - 126.

20. Renn, 1964   D. F. Renn, Potters and Kilns in Medieval Hertfordshire, Hertfordshire Local History Council Publications (1964).